ON
FAITH

ON
FAITH

LESSONS FROM AN
AMERICAN BELIEVER

ANTONIN
SCALIA

EDITED BY CHRISTOPHER J. SCALIA
AND EDWARD WHELAN

CROWN
FORUM
NEW YORK

All rights reserved.
Published in the United States by Crown Forum, an imprint of
the Crown Publishing Group, a division of Penguin Random
House LLC, New York.
crownpublishing.com

CROWN FORUM with colophon is a registered trademark of
Penguin Random House LLC.

Grateful acknowledgment is made to the following for
permission to reprint previously published materials:

First Things: "God's Justice and Ours" by Justice Antonin
Scalia, published by *First Things* (www.firstthings.com) May 2002,
and "Funeral Homily for Justice Antonin Scalia" by Rev. Paul
D. Scalia, published by *First Things* (www.firstthings.com)
February 22, 2016. Used by permission of First Things. All rights
reserved.

National Review, Inc.: "Latin and Greek" by Father Robert
Connor excerpted from "Antonin Scalia—A Justice in Full"
published by *National Review* February 29, 2016, copyright ©
2016 by National Review, Inc. Used by permission of National
Review, Inc. All rights reserved.

Library of Congress Cataloging-in-Publication Data is available.

ISBN 978-1-9848-2331-1
Ebook ISBN 978-1-9848-2332-8

Printed in the United States of America

Jacket design by Lucas Heinrich

10 9 8 7 6 5 4 3 2 1

First Edition

To Maureen Scalia

Why, it's a lion I married! A lion! A lion!
—*A Man for All Seasons*

CONTENTS

EDITORS' NOTE

———————

As the double meaning of the subtitle suggests, this volume collects Justice Scalia's thoughts both about religious belief and about the place of religion in American public life. It comprises some of his many efforts, as a faithful Catholic and proud American, to inspire and guide others in their faith and citizenship, and to explain the freedoms that the Constitution grants, as well as the limitations it places, on religious expression. The collection includes speeches, excerpts from some of his Supreme Court opinions, and reflections on his faith by his friends, colleagues, law clerks, and family.

All but one of the speeches in this collection were previously collected in the *New York Times* bestseller *Scalia Speaks: Reflections on Law, Faith, and Life Well Lived* (Crown Forum). We have given most of those speeches different titles for this book to accommodate their new context and to clarify the collection's thematic framework.

For ease of reading, we have sometimes omitted internal citations and ellipses and have occasionally changed capitalization and punctuation, but we have often retained Justice Scalia's distinctive use of commas and semicolons.

With one exception, all of the personal reflections are published here for the first time.

Justice Scalia had done preliminary work on a collection of his religious speeches before his untimely death. It is our honor to have expanded and completed his project; it is our hope that this book gives you a deeper appreciation of his faith in God and his love for his country.

—CJS & EW

FOREWORD

BY JUSTICE CLARENCE THOMAS

I was truly blessed to have had Nino at the Court when I became a member. And I was blessed many times over the almost twenty-five years that we served together.

There were countless chats walking to chambers after oral arguments or after our conferences. Those very brief visits usually involved more laughter than anything else. There were the many buck-each-other-up visits or checking on each other after one of us had an unpleasant experience. And there were calls to test an idea or work through a problem.

Nino worked hard to get things right—the broad principles and the details of law, grammar, syntax, and vocabulary. He was passionate about it all; all deserved and received his full attention. I loved the eagerness and satisfaction in his voice when he finished a writing with which he was particularly pleased. "Clarence, you have got to hear this. It is really good." Whereupon he would deliver a dramatic reading.

For the last few years of his life, my place on the bench was between Nino and Steve Breyer. I loved the back-and-forth that took place, especially the passing of notes and the whispered or muttered commentary. When Nino wanted to talk quietly with me about something, he would lean far back in his chair and say in an almost endearing tone, "Brother Clarence, what do you think . . . ?"

Nino did not discuss his faith with me often, but his deep belief in God was implicit in everything he did.

In today's world, it's easy to mouth platitudes about one's faith without taking corresponding actions. I don't recall Nino ever doing so. He made it clear that practicing his faith was important, but never in a trite way. If anything, I would occasionally hear him chide himself for not attending daily Mass and praise his wife, Maureen, for doing so. But he was not showy or flamboyant about his faith. For Nino, it was what he did and how he did it—his dedication both to his vocation as a judge and to his beloved family—that spoke loudly for him.

Nino's faith was robust, deeply personal, and central to his life—it guided him and gave structure to his life. It led him to love and care well for his family. And it fueled a deep commitment to his judicial oath and the duties and obligations that it entailed. This is what I saw on a day-to-day basis. His Catholic faith helped him to understand that he had no right or license to exceed his judicial authority or to abdicate his responsibilities; it imposed a constant judicial modesty or humility. He would be violating his oath if he imposed his personal views on others under the guise of a judicial opinion, and he had no inherent or personal right to judge his fellow man. Rather, his only authority was his limited role as an Article III judge, and he had given his word to Almighty God to comport himself consistent with this limited grant of authority.

One need only read his opinions to see this discipline and restraint. The effort that he put into each opinion was not for personal vanity or aggrandizement. It was not for manufacturing a legacy. Rather, it was because his oath, which rested on the foundations of his faith, required him to give his all.

Likewise, he would also violate his oath if he withheld a legitimate judicial opinion that might upset others—even those he loved. He was required to do his absolute best in each case, to be honest with himself and with others, no matter how difficult, no matter if it led to disagreements. In the end, God was watching and would be the final Judge, and it was to Him alone that he would give an account. To the very end, upholding his oath is precisely what he did.

When our work was particularly challenging and the burdens seemed oppressive, I would occasionally drop in to visit him in his office. In short order, it was always clear that he would soldier on—his faith and commitment to God required that he do so.

In a sense, it was providential (and certainly not probable) that we would serve together. When I joined the Court, I only knew of him but had never met him. He was from the Northeast, while I am from the Southeast. He came from a house of educators, I from a household of almost no formal education. But we shared our Catholic faith and our Jesuit education as well as our sense of vocation. Our faith mattered, and so it was that our work had to matter and had to be done right.

For different reasons and from different origins, we were heading in the same direction. So we walked together and worked together for a quarter century. And along the way we developed an unbreakable bond of trust and deep affection. Many have fittingly, deservedly, and rightfully said much about his intellect and jurisprudence. But there is so much more to this good man. As one of our colleagues said, he filled the room. His passion and his sense of humor were always on full display.

And so was his love for Maureen, his family, his Church, our country, and our Constitution.

Shortly after Nino's death, I finished reading Eric Metaxas's biography of Dietrich Bonhoeffer. One of Hitler's last acts before the Allies defeated Germany was to have this man of God executed. I thought of Nino as I read the eulogy of Bonhoeffer delivered by a close friend of his. With apologies, I borrow liberally: "'With him a piece of my own life is carried to the grave.' Yet: our eyes are upon Thee. We believe in the communion of saints, the forgiveness of sins, the resurrection of the body and the life everlasting. We give thanks to God for the life, the suffering, the witness of our brother whose friends we were privileged to be. We pray God to lead us, too, through his discipleship from this world into His heavenly kingdom; to fulfill in us [Bonhoeffer's conviction]: *'non potest non laetari qui sperat in Dominum'*—'while in God confiding I cannot but rejoice.'"

God bless you, Brother Nino. God bless you!

Introduction

A Different Kind of Devout

BY REV. PAUL D. SCALIA

In a conversation several months before his death, my father abruptly told me, "I've been praying the Rosary every morning on my way into the office." He said it in his brusque, matter-of-fact, even challenging manner. I was stunned—not that he would pray the Rosary but that he would speak about his prayer life at all. That was not his way. Wanting to encourage him in this good practice, I stammered some brilliant priestly counsel: "That's great, Dad." "Yeah?" he shot back. "Do you think it does any damn good?" I pointed out the theological truth that, no, with that attitude it probably doesn't. He laughed, our conversation moved on, and that brief glimpse of his devotion was gone. His point was made, and so was mine.

My father's answer should not be taken as an expression of doubt about the power of prayer, though he shared a frustration common to all believers: he struggled to understand why God did not seem to answer prayers in a timely manner, or sometimes at all. His abruptness and deflection came from a different place, from a discomfort and reticence in speaking about his prayer life. As much as Dad spoke about the Catholic faith, often publicly, he rarely spoke about his personal faith. Today's emphasis on giving a personal witness or speaking about one's faith journey would have been foreign to him. As far as he was concerned, what mattered was not his faith but The Faith.

For years I have heard my father referred to as a "devout" Catholic. I always wince at that word, which typically describes one who comes easily to his religious practice, prays peacefully, and speaks naturally about his faith. That wasn't my father. He was indeed a man of faith and, in his own way, devout. But like everything else in his life, faith had something of an argument and contest about it. After all, this was the man who, when asked by reporters about how he responds to those who question his public practice of faith, made a dismissive (misinterpreted by some as obscene) Italian gesture *on his way out of Mass.*

My father was devout in his own rough-and-tumble manner. He practiced the faith, but he didn't think his own example worth imitating or his own spiritual life worth speaking about. He believed what the Church taught, treasured the Mass, confessed his sins, and attended retreats. But grace before meals was always a quick-run thing, the drive to Sunday Mass was helter-skelter, and his opinion about music and sermons (*never* "homilies") was unvarnished.

He would call fairly regularly to ask me to offer Mass for an ill or deceased friend of his. The first of many exchanges was indicative:

DAD: "Don Paolo, I want to buy a Mass."

ME: [sigh] "Dad, you can't *buy* a Mass."

DAD: [exasperated] "I know *that*! But . . . well, you know what I *mean*! I want you to say a Mass for someone!"

On future calls he would deliberately ask to "buy a Mass"—to keep the joke going and, no doubt, to get under my skin. His asking to have Masses offered was certainly devout . . . but not in the usual sense.

Over the years we did catch occasional glimpses of a piety that his gruff, contrarian exterior typically concealed. On one occasion he told me about a powerful experience from his childhood. While at Boy Scout camp, he rose early one morning for Mass. He arrived at the chapel to find no one else there except the priest and the altar boy. That was, he explained, when the Mass started to take hold of him. He was struck that the Mass was of such importance that the priest would offer it even if no one else came.

On another occasion, one weekday afternoon, he loaded all of us (however many were at home) into the van and drove us to the local parish to pray for a dying friend. The trip stands out in my mind precisely because it was so unusual. Church was for Sundays and holy days of obligation, not random weekday afternoons. Although most details of that brief visit escape me, I do remember him kneeling in prayer, and in tears. Another moment that comes to mind is when he walked my sister Mary and me through Saint Ignatius of Loyola's demanding prayer of abandonment, the Suscipe. He spoke passionately about how much he liked it and yet how difficult he found it to pray.

That is what we witnessed growing up. Dad was a Catholic living a dogged fidelity to the Church's teachings and Sacraments. He did so, imperfectly but perseveringly. He practiced the faith, but he didn't think his own example worth imitating or his own spiritual life worth speaking about. One time, after my brothers and I had been irreverent at Mass, he gave us a well-deserved scolding. It was not a personal reflection on what the Eucharist meant to him in his faith journey, but a firm and heartfelt lecture on what the Mass *is*.

When I was appointed pastor of my family's old parish, I was blessed to have him attend Mass there regularly. Of course, I see the blessing only in retrospect. He could be demanding. He desired clear and faithful sermons, good music, and Latin properly pronounced. And he was not shy in letting a priest know when one of these was lacking. In fact, the summer before my ordination to the priesthood, I had jokingly informed him that he would not be allowed to attend my Masses for precisely this reason. He was shocked by my ban and blurted out: "But . . . but I want to kibitz!"

Years later, and despite my prohibition, there he was every Sunday. And it was a blessing. Yes, he was free with his suggestions about what I could do differently. And on more than one occasion he generously shared his unsolicited thoughts on discipline with the parents of unruly children. But these things were in the background. The blessing that emerged was to observe his devotion in a different way—no longer as a boy, but as a grown man and as a priest.

He still had the old Latin hand missal that he had always brought to Mass. Such a book was standard years ago. It contained the readings and prayers for Mass in Latin and English, side by side, and other devotional prayers. His was well worn. He had bought his copy in 1960, the year he married my mother. The page ribbons had long since broken off. Holy cards from fifty years of funerals, retreats, and anniversaries served as bookmarks. The missal had lost much of its usefulness when the Mass was changed in 1970, but he still knew how to make the most of it. He knew exactly where to find his favorite prayers and readings.

In 2007, the Traditional Latin Mass (or "Extraordinary Form," as it is officially termed) became more widely available in the Catholic Church. Suddenly that old missal had a new lease on life, as Dad typically came to the Traditional Latin Mass. It was the Mass of his childhood, youth, and first years of marriage. At that Mass the faithful kneel at the Communion rail to receive Holy Communion. As they kneel, the priest walks along the rail and places the Host on their tongues. There is something wonderfully democratic about the Communion rail. It is no respecter of persons and reveals the fundamental equality of all God's children. Everyone must adopt the same humble posture of kneeling. At the Communion rail the great variety of Christ's faithful—rich and poor, learned and ignorant, old and young—kneel side by side, with no regard for their differences. The priest often encounters people shoulder to shoulder who would never otherwise be found together. So it was that I frequently found my powerful father—a "Supreme Justice," as he liked to joke—kneeling next to, well, anyone. Perhaps the little girl who just made her First Communion, or the harried mother of a large family, or the out-of-work father, or the clerk from the grocery store. In short, next to ordinary people who neither knew nor cared about his important office. Dad appreciated that in the Church it didn't matter how much he had accomplished or attained. As a Catholic he knelt for the Lord, like all the rest.

"Here comes everybody" was James Joyce's description of the Catholic Church. Wrong about many things, he got this one right. That the Church is *catholic* means that she is universal; that she draws all kinds of people, and for all kinds of reasons. One person is drawn by the Church's social doctrine and service of the poor, another by her missionary zeal. For one it is her liturgy, for another her moral teachings. For my father, it was the integrity and clarity of the Church's teachings.

Catholicism requires the investment of the entire person. It engages not just the will and the passions, but also the intellect. "You shall love the Lord your God with all your heart, and with all your soul, *and with all your mind*" (Matthew 22:37). We are to be "transformed by the renewal of the mind" (Romans 12:2). In practice, however, many believers have accepted a false dichotomy between faith and reason. Because the truths of faith are beyond the mind's ability to grasp fully—hence the Catholic Church calls them "mysteries"—people consider them disconnected from or even opposed to human reason. In many churches, faith has become the realm of feelings; thought is checked at the door. This quickly makes liturgy mere sentimentality and doctrine a matter of opinion. One of my greatest frustrations as a priest is not that people ask questions, but that they do not ask more of them. It is astounding how otherwise intelligent people willingly suspend their minds in matters of faith.

My father made no such division between faith and reason. He understood that the act of faith does not mean the end of thought. His library (which I had been plundering for years) reflected this. It was full of authors who combined genuine piety and clear thinking: Augustine, Aquinas, Newman, Belloc, Chesterton, Lewis, etc. I remember one Lent speaking with him about Cardinal John Henry Newman's discourse *The Mental Sufferings of Our Lord in His Passion*. He loved the way Newman united the exercise of the mind with the devotion of the heart. The two were not opposed but meant to complement each other.

My father expected the same intellectual honesty and clarity from the Church's pastors. A priest did not have to preach with the intellectual depth of Cardinal Newman, but he should at least speak with reverence for and confidence in the Church's teachings. Suspension of thought in favor of religious platitudes was bad.

Lazy reasoning that deformed doctrine was worse. There was one stock homily phrase that always merited particular condemnation: "In a special way . . ." Those words, in Dad's estimation, signaled either fuzzy thinking or just plain sentimentality—neither of which was acceptable. We were all on the alert for that phrase from the pulpit and grinned knowingly when it came.

At the same time, his insistence on clear thinking did not lead him to intellectualize religious practice. Dad understood that salvation comes through faith, not through thought. He defended simple, seemingly naive faith against an intellectual elitism. Indeed, he delighted in coming to the defense of those believers the *Washington Post* once called "largely poor, uneducated, and easy to command." His famous "Not to the Wise" speech was one such example, as was his mischievous baiting of an incredulous *New York Magazine* reporter with talk about Satan: "I even believe in the Devil. . . . Of course! Yeah, he's a real person. Hey, c'mon, that's standard Catholic doctrine! Every Catholic believes that. . . . If you are faithful to Catholic dogma, that is certainly a large part of it."

Dad was devout according to both faith and reason. He liked to "kibitz" about the faith. Many times he came up to me after Mass, excited about some particular phrasing of a prayer or translation of a passage, jabbing his finger at the relevant text in his missal, wanting to discuss its meaning. Just moments before he had been kneeling in his pew after receiving Holy

Communion, recollecting himself, giving thanks to God, and thumbing through that same missal for the perfect prayer of faith.

Dad also treasured the Church's beauty. Some years ago, then-Cardinal Ratzinger (later Pope Benedict XVI) observed that one of the most convincing demonstrations of the Catholic Church's truth is "the beauty that the faith has generated." That statement by a man of such intellectual standing might surprise us because we tend to associate beauty with feelings and not with truth. Dad would have understood it immediately. He was a cultured man and appreciated beauty at the opera, at the symphony, and in museums. But he appreciated the Church's patrimony of beauty—her architecture, sculptures, paintings, and music—not only as an aesthetic phenomenon, but as an expression of her truth. He understood that truth and beauty are two different but complementary ways of expressing the Catholic faith. This is one reason he was drawn to the Traditional Latin Mass. He found that the beauty of its ancient rituals, chants, and prayers provided a particularly strong expression of the Church's faith.

When I was ordained a priest in 1996, Dad had been on the Court for a decade. By that time, he had become a coveted speaker for Catholic and other religious groups throughout the country. Although he abhorred the idea of his being a "Catholic jurist" or that there was a peculiarly Catholic way of reading the Constitution, he gladly spoke about faith and its importance in our nation's life. As he told me the summer of my ordination, he considered his giving such speeches to be an apostolate, an opportunity to build up others in faith.

My father understood that because of his position he had an opportunity to encourage others by his own religious practice and candid words about faith. He saw this witness as a responsibility not only as a Catholic but also as an American. Over the past fifty years our culture has privatized religion, sidelined it from public life. This segregation takes a toll on the believer, making him feel like a misfit in his own nation. More importantly for my father, the privatization of religion is out of keeping with our nation's founding and strongest traditions. Dad knew and appreciated our nation's historical dependence on a religious citizenry. He wanted to do his part to encourage believers.

Only after his death did I learn how right he was. I was overwhelmed by the number of people—from all religions, from all over the world—who expressed thanks for his witness to faith in the public square. That a man of such stature and intellectual caliber would present himself also as a believer moved them to take their faith more seriously and live it more boldly. It was a great consolation to learn that his faith, which had always guided and inspired me, had also helped many others. Dad was unapologetically Catholic. But his open witness to the Catholic faith inspired believers of every kind.

Father Scalia is a priest of the Diocese of Arlington, Virginia, where he serves as Episcopal Vicar for Clergy.

PART I

PERSONAL LESSONS
FOR CHRISTIANS

Not to the Wise—the Christian as Cretin

How can intelligent Christians exercise their faith in a skeptical world? How can they reconcile reason and faith? To address these questions, Justice Scalia considered the perspectives of two great men named Thomas. Perhaps surprisingly given Scalia's admiration for the American founding, Thomas Jefferson served as a negative example, as he viewed belief in miracles as "vulgar ignorance." Justice Scalia contrasted Jefferson with St. Thomas More, the lord high chancellor of England who was executed for respecting the Pope's authority to refuse King Henry VIII's divorce. Because he saw with the eyes of faith, this learned man of reason was regarded as a fool by his friends and even by his wife.

St. Thomas More, the patron saint of lawyers, was a hero to Justice Scalia, who delivered the following speech to religious audiences around the country.

The title of my talk today is "Not to the Wise—the Christian as Cretin." The second half of that title, "The Christian as Cretin," is meant, of course, to be a play on words. And it is a wordplay that has some etymological basis. The English word *cretin*, meaning "a person of deficient mental capacity," in fact derives from the

French word *chrétien*, meaning "Christian," which was used in the Middle Ages to refer to the short, often grotesque, severely retarded people who were to be found in some remote valleys of the Alps—perhaps the result of excessive inbreeding. These people were called *chrétiens*—Christians—to make the point that they were human souls and not brutes.

It has often occurred to me, however, that for quite different reasons the equivalence of the words *Christian* and *cretin* makes a lot of sense. To be honest about it, that is the view of Christians—or at least of traditional Christians—taken by sophisticated society in modern times. One can be sophisticated and believe in God—heck, a First Mover is at least as easy to believe in as a Big Bang triggered by nothingness. One can even be sophisticated and believe in a *personal* God, a benevolent Being who loves mankind, so long as that Being does not intrude too ridiculously into the world—by working so-called miracles, for example, or by limiting human behavior in inconvenient ways. And one can even be sophisticated and believe in Jesus Christ, as having been in some sense a "son" of God (are we not all children of the Creator?) and as having in some sense triumphed over death (his message, after all, lives on). One can believe all that, I say, and still be considered sophisticated.

But to believe in what might be called "traditional" Christianity is something else. To believe, first and foremost, that Jesus Christ *was God*. (Why, the notion that the Creator should become a man is as unsophisticated as the notion that Zeus should become a bull.) Or to believe that he was born of a virgin. (Well, I mean, really!) That he actually, physically, rose from the grave. That he founded a church with power to bind and loose—to pronounce, authoritatively, the will of God for mankind. That, as he taught, hardship and suffering are not to be avoided at all costs but are to be embraced and indeed even sought after—as penance for sin, and as a means of sharing in the crucifixion of Christ. (How utterly ridiculous to forgo perfectly legitimate pleasures, and to seek discomfort! How absurd the vow of chastity and the hair shirt!) Or the belief in miracles, as at Lourdes or Fatima. Or, finally, the belief that those who love God and obey his commands will rise from the dead, in their bodies, and be happy with him forever in heaven; and that those who do not will burn eternally in hell.

Surely those who adhere to all or most of these traditional Christian beliefs are regarded, within the educated circles that you and I travel in, as—well, simpleminded. The attitude of the wise is well reflected in the statement that appeared in a news story (not an opinion piece) in the *Washington Post* some years ago, stating, matter-of-factly (as though anyone of intelligence knew and agreed with it), that Christian fundamentalists were "largely poor, uneducated and easy to command." The same attitude applies, of course, to traditional Catholics—by which I mean those who do such positively peasant-like things as saying the rosary, kneeling in adoration before the Eucharist, going on pilgrimages to Lourdes or Fatima, and, worst of all, following *indiscriminately* (rather than in smorgasbord fashion) the teachings of the Church. Surely these people are "uneducated and easy to command." *Chrétien*, cretin.

Let me turn now to the first part of my title: "Not to the Wise." I mean that as an allusion to the Gospel passage that you and I have heard read at Mass frequently. As recorded by St. Matthew and St. Luke, Christ said: "I praise thee, Father, Lord of heaven and earth, that thou didst hide these things from the wise and prudent, and didst reveal them to little ones." The same thought appears many other times in the New Testament. St. Paul writes to the Corinthians that "the natural man [i.e., the man of the world] does not perceive the things that are of the Spirit of God, for it is foolishness to him and he cannot understand." And he advises them: "Let no one deceive himself. If any one of you thinks himself wise in this world, let him become a fool, that he may come to be wise. For the wisdom of this world is foolishness with God." In other words, St. Paul quite entirely expected—he *assumed*— that the wise of the world would regard Christians as fools. And from the beginning until now that expectation has not been disappointed.

It is interesting to read of St. Paul's experience in that ancient center of wisdom and intellectuality, Athens. The Acts of the Apostles record some great successes in Paul's preaching; Athens was not one of them. He goes to the Areopagus—where, as the Acts contemptuously describe it, "all the Athenians and the visitors there from abroad used to spend all their leisure telling or listening to something new." Sort of an open-air *Donahue Show*, though perhaps a bit more intellectually elevated. Anyway, Paul goes up there, and he has this really clever speech laid out, in which he says that he knows the people of Athens are very religious, and he has noticed that one of their altars is inscribed "To the Unknown God." It is that God he has come to tell them about. This is a brilliant intro, and Paul gets rolling along pretty well, until he says that this God he has been talking about "will judge the world with justice by a Man whom he has appointed, and whom he has guaranteed to all by raising him from the dead." Well, that breaks it. The wise men of Athens, circa A.D. 50, know just as well as the wise men of America, A.D. 2010, that people don't rise from the dead. As the Acts record it: "Now when they heard of a resurrection of the dead, some began to sneer, but others said, 'We will hear thee again on this matter.'" Paul did not think the prospects of their hearing him again good enough to be worth his time. The next line of the Acts is "So Paul went forth from among them."

Now let me propel you forward in time, from A.D. 50 to A.D. 1804—just yesterday, by comparison—to the study of another wise man, a worthy successor of those of Athens and one of our nation's greatest political figures, Thomas Jefferson. Jefferson is creating the work that he would call *The Life and Morals of Jesus of Nazareth*, known more familiarly as the Jefferson Bible. As one historian [Jaroslav Pelikan] describes the scene:

> There has certainly never been a shortage of boldness in the history of biblical scholarship during the past two centuries, but for sheer audacity Thomas Jefferson's two redactions of the Gospels stand out even in that company. It is still a bit overwhelming to contemplate the sangfroid exhibited by the third president of the United States as, razor in hand, he sat editing the Gospels during February 1804, on (as he himself says) "2. or 3. nights only at Washington, after getting thro' the evening task of reading the letters and papers of the day." He was apparently quite sure that he could tell what was genuine and what was not in the transmitted text of the New Testament.

No problema for a wise man. As Jefferson described the process in one of his letters:

> *We find in the writings of [Jesus's] biographers [i.e., the Evangelists] matter of two distinct descriptions. First, a groundwork of vulgar ignorance, of things impossible, of superstitions, fanaticisms and fabrications. Intermixed with these, again, are sublime ideas of the Supreme Being, aphorisms and precepts of the purest morality and benevolence, sanctioned by a*

life of humility, innocence and simplicity of manners,
neglect of riches, absence of worldly ambition and
honors, with an eloquence and persuasiveness
which have not been surpassed. These could not be
inventions of the groveling authors who related them.
They are far beyond the powers of their feeble minds.
They show that there was a character, the subject of
their history, whose splendid conceptions were above
all suspicion of being interpolations from their hands.
Can we be at a loss in separating such materials, and
ascribing each to its genuine author? The difference is
obvious to the eye and to the understanding, and we
may read as we run to each his part; and I will venture
to affirm, that he who, as I have done, will undertake
to winnow this grain from the chaff, will find it not
to require a moment's consideration. The parts fall
asunder of themselves, as would those of an image of
metal and clay.

In another letter, Jefferson said, "I separate . . . the gold from the dross; restore to [Jesus] the former, and leave the latter to the stupidity of some, and roguery of others of his disciples."

Well, the product of this exegesis is easy to imagine. It is a gospel fit for the Age of Reason—or indeed, for the wise of any age, including our own. I will satisfy your curiosity with examples from the beginning and the end. Jefferson's Bible does not begin with the betrothal of Joseph and Mary, the Annunciation by the angel Gabriel, the conception by the Holy Spirit.

It begins with the decree from Caesar Augustus, the married couple Joseph and Mary going down to Bethlehem, and Jesus's birth in the stable. There are a few changes from the version you and I are familiar with. No shepherds in the fields, no multitude of the heavenly host, no wise men from the East, no slaughter of the innocents, no flight into Egypt. From Bethlehem, Joseph and Mary take the kid right back to Nazareth. As for the ending of the Jefferson Bible, I will read it to you:

> Now, in the place where he was crucified, there was a garden; and in the garden a new sepulchre, wherein was never man yet laid. There laid they Jesus, and rolled a great stone to the door of the sepulchre, and departed.

Cut. End of story. Run the crawl. As I told you earlier, the wise do not believe in resurrection of the dead (it is really quite absurd), just as they do not believe in virgin birth—so everything from Easter morning to the Ascension had to have been made up by those "groveling authors," those "rogues" Jefferson referred to, presumably part of their clever plan to get themselves crucified.

My point is not that reason and intellect must be laid aside where matters of religion are concerned. Assuredly not. A faith that has no rational basis is a false faith. That is why I am not a Branch Davidian. It is not irrational, however, to accept the testimony of eyewitnesses, who had nothing to gain by dissembling, about the resurrection of Jesus Christ, and about what Jesus taught them; or, for that matter, to accept the evidence of later miracles that establish the truth of the Church that Christ founded. What *is* irrational, it seems to me, is to reject *a priori*, with no investigation, the possibility of miracles in general, and of Jesus Christ's resurrection in particular—which is, of course, precisely what the worldly-wise do. They just will not have anything to do with miracles.

There was some excitement in the Washington area some years ago concerning a local priest who was said to have the stigmata, and in whose presence statues of the Virgin Mary and of the saints were said to weep. It didn't seem right. Stuff like that was supposed to happen in little villages in Italy or Portugal or Mexico—not inside the Beltway, for Pete's sake! (I felt sorry for our bishop, of course. Surely there can be nothing more difficult than having putative miracles occurring in your diocese. It's a no-win situation. In the histories of the great saints and visionaries, the local bishop, whose job is to be skeptical, is often the heavy—but never, as I recall, the hero.) Anyway, the *Washington Post* sent out a team of reporters, who produced a strange story about the phenomenon of these weeping statues: they obviously did not want to appear so unsophisticated as to believe this nonsense, but neither could they find any explanation for it. As far as they could tell, the young priest was not a charlatan, and puddles of water did indeed appear at the feet of the statues.

Well, I did not drive the few miles over to check it out; one more miracle is not going to make me believe any more than I already do. But the thought occurred to me: Why wasn't that church absolutely packed with non-believers seeking to determine whether there might be something to this Catholic religion? Or why weren't the *Washington Post* reporters enthusiastic converts? Well, of course, the wisdom of the world does not operate that way. The wise do not investigate such silliness—and even if the miracle were performed under their nose, they would disbelieve. You may re-call the parable of Dives, the rich man, and Lazarus the beggar who used to sit by his gate. When they die, Lazarus goes to heaven and Dives to hell. Dives prays to Abraham to send Lazarus to his brothers—to warn them, "lest they also come into this place of torment." But Abraham says, "They have Moses and the proph-ets; let them hear them," to which Dives replies, "Nay, father Abraham: but if one went unto them from the dead, they will repent." And Abraham rejoins: "If they hear not Moses and prophets, neither will they be per-suaded, though one rose from the dead." Quite so.

I have spoken to this lawyers' group (unflatteringly, sad to say) about one lawyer who was something of a universal man, Thomas Jefferson. To demonstrate what I mean about the intelligent Christian's appear-ing stupid to the world, let me say a few words about another lawyer–universal man: the patron saint of this organization, St. Thomas More. His life, or more precisely the ending of his life, is the prime example of the Christian as cretin.

More was, of course, one of the great men of his age: lawyer, scholar, humanist, philosopher, statesman—a towering figure not just in his own country of England but throughout Renaissance Europe. You will have missed the deep significance of More's martyrdom—and you will not understand why More is a particularly apt patron saint for lawyers, scholars, and intellectuals—unless you appreciate that the reason he died was, in the view of almost everyone at the time, a silly one. Many martyrs have died for refusing to deny Jesus Christ, or for spreading his Gospel, or for adhering to his clear moral teachings. In going to their death, they have had the comfort of knowing that their Christian predecessors, contemporaries, and successors would praise and approve their obstinacy. Thomas More, on the other hand, went to his death to support the proposition that only the Bishop of Rome could bind or loose the marriage of Henry VIII. A papacy corrupt and politicized. A papacy that often granted or withheld divorce for reasons of diplomacy rather than doctrine—which may well have been the case with regard to the denial of Henry's divorce. More knew all that. More himself, like his humanist contemporaries such as Erasmus, had been a harsh critic of Rome.

Hilaire Belloc, in a lovely little essay on More entitled "The Witness to Abstract Truth," describes the situation like this:

After four hundred years we have to-day forgotten how the matter looked to the men of the early sixteenth century. The average Englishman had little concern with the quarrel between the Crown and Rome. It did not touch his life. The Mass went on just the same and all the splendour of religion; the monasteries were still in being everywhere, there was no interruption whatsoever. Most of the great bodies—all the bishops except Fisher—had yielded. They had not yielded with great reluctance but as a matter of course. . . . To the ordinary man of that day, anyone, especially a highly placed official, who stood out against the King's policy *was a crank*.

In what he did, More was unsupported by intelligent society, by his friends, even by his own wife. Robert Bolt's play *A Man for All Seasons* puts that point nicely. When More learns that the convocation of bishops has voted unanimously (except for John Fisher of Rochester) to adhere to the king's demands that they acknowledge his divorce despite the Pope, More decides that he must resign the chancellorship, and he asks his wife, Alice, to help him remove his chain of office. She says: "Sun and moon, Master More, you're taken for a wise man! Is this wisdom—to betray your ability, abandon practice, forget your station and your duty to your kin and behave like a printed book!" And later along the road, his friend the Duke of Norfolk says: "You're behaving like a fool. You're behaving like a crank. You're not behaving like a gentleman. . . . [I]t's disproportionate! . . . [W]e've all given in! Why must you stand out?" Foolish and disproportionate indeed. As one biographer put it, "More died for a Papacy that, as far as men could see, was little else than a small Italian princedom ruled by some of the least reputable of the Renaissance princes."

But of course More was seeing not with the eyes of men, but with the eyes of faith. He believed Christ's word that Peter was the Rock, and the Christian tradition that the Pope was the head of the Church. As low as the papacy had declined (one does not get much lower than Alexander VI, who reigned during More's lifetime), the Vicar of Christ alone—and not all the bishops of England—had the power to bind and to loose. I find it hard to understand the reasoning of those wise people who revere Thomas More as a saint rather than a world-class fool for dying to support the decision of Medici Pope Clement VII concerning King Henry's divorce of Catherine of Aragon, but who themselves ignore and indeed positively oppose the teachings of Pope John Paul II on much more traditional and less politically charged subjects. Go figure.

It is the hope of most speakers to impart wisdom. It has been my hope to impart, to those already wise in Christ, the courage to have their wisdom regarded as stupidity. Are we thought to be fools? No doubt. But, as St. Paul wrote to the Corinthians, "We are fools for Christ's sake." And are we thought to be "easily led" and childish? Well, Christ did constantly describe us as, of all things, his sheep, and said we would not get to heaven unless we became like little children. For the courage to suffer the contempt of the sophisticated world for these seeming failings of ours, we lawyers and intellectuals—who do not like to be regarded as unsophisticated—can have no greater model than the patron of this society, the great, intellectual, urbane, foolish, childish man that he was. St. Thomas More, pray for us.

A Prayer by St. Thomas More

When Justice Scalia delivered "Not to the Wise," he always made sure to have with him this prayer that St. Thomas More composed while imprisoned in the Tower of London awaiting his execution.

Give me the grace, Good Lord,

To set the world at naught. To set the mind firmly on You and not to hang upon the words of men's mouths.

To be content to be solitary. Not to long for worldly pleasures. Little by little utterly to cast off the world and rid my mind of all its business.

Not to long to hear of earthly things, but that the hearing of worldly fancies may be displeasing to me.

Gladly to be thinking of God, piteously to call for His help. To lean into the comfort of God. Busily to labor to love Him.

To know my own vileness and wretchedness. To humble myself under the mighty hand of God. To bewail my sins and, for the purging of them, patiently to suffer adversity.

Gladly to bear my purgatory here. To be joyful in tribulations. To walk the narrow way that leads to life.

To have the last thing in remembrance. To have ever

before my eyes my death that is ever at hand. To make death no stranger to me. To foresee and consider the everlasting fire of Hell. To pray for pardon before the judge comes.

To have continually in mind the passion that Christ suffered for me. For His benefits unceasingly to give Him thanks.

To buy the time again that I have lost. To abstain from vain conversations. To shun foolish mirth and gladness. To cut off unnecessary recreations.

Of worldly substance, friends, liberty, life and all, to set the loss at naught, for the winning of Christ.

To think my worst enemies my best friends, for the brethren of Joseph could never have done him so much good with their love and favor as they did him with their malice and hatred.

These minds are more to be desired of every man than all the treasures of all the princes and kings, Christian and heathen, were it gathered and laid together all in one heap.

Amen.

On Being Different—the Christian as Pilgrim

In this 1992 speech, Justice Scalia reflected on the "apartness" he felt growing up as a Catholic—an apartness that the Catholic Church seemed to encourage through its practices and traditions, and which reminded the faithful "that the ways of Christ and the ways of the world . . . are not the same, and we should not expect them to be." This sense of difference in little things helps one develop the strength necessary to follow Christ's teachings and underscores "the divergence of Christian teaching from the morality of the general society"—a divergence as old as Christianity itself.

The announced topic for my talk today was "On Being Different." I am sure many of you come here today thinking to learn how or why in the world I can write these eight-to-one dissents, or not believe in substantive due process. In fact, however, I intend to speak not about being different in the law (a relatively unimportant subject), but rather about being different in life. More specifically, I want to speak about the expectation—the reality—that Christians will be different.

I and those Catholics in the room who are my age or older have had the great good fortune of growing up at a time when even in areas with large Catholic populations such as New York or Chicago, it was a little bit strange to be a Catholic. Catholic was not "mainstream." There were still some places where Catholics, like Jews, were not welcome. America had not yet had a Catholic president. John F. Kennedy had not yet appeared to express the hope that his fellow citizens would not vote against him "because," as he put it, "of my religious affiliation."

I have always hated that phrase, reducing the most profound commitment of a man's life to a mere membership preference. "Ah, yes, I am a Catholic. But I might be a Muslim or a Jew or even an Episcopalian tomorrow, if I should choose to change my 'religious affiliation.'" Perhaps there is an open season, like changing from Blue Cross to the Postal Worker's Plan. Surely the man should have said, "I hope no one will vote against me because of what I am." That is what my hero Popeye would have said. "I yam what I yam." But never mind.

My point, before I launched myself into this digression, is that when I was growing up, to be Catholic was to be a bit different. It was a little bit beyond—in some parts of the country a lot beyond—what was respectable.

And the Church, I must say, far from seeking to eliminate that differentness, in some ways seemed to go out of its way to emphasize it. The Protestants here may remember that their Catholic friends used to have to eat fish on Fridays, when everyone else was having hot dogs. And at a Saturday-night party the Catholics (or at least those who planned to receive Communion the next day) would no longer eat or drink anything after midnight. These dietary rules were not as strict, or as noticeable, as those observed by, for example, Orthodox Jews. But they still served to increase rather than reduce our "apartness."

Now, there were many bad aspects to that "apartness." It kept us Catholics, for example, from participating in the kind of fellowship with men and women of other Christian faiths we are enjoying here this morning. But there were some good aspects as well—and aspects that are sorely missed, I think, in modern Christianity. That "differentness" said to me in the field of religion what my parents repeatedly reminded me of in the field of social activity. Whenever I wanted to go to a certain movie, or a certain place, that my parents disapproved of, I would say, of course, as children always do, that everybody else was going. My parents' invariable and unanswerable response was: "You're not everybody else."

It is enormously important, I think, for Christians to learn early and remember long that lesson of "differentness"; to recognize that what is perfectly lawful, and perfectly permissible, for everyone else—even our very close non-Christian friends—is not necessarily lawful and permissible for us. That the ways of Christ and the ways of the world—even the world of Main Street America—are not the same, and we should not expect them to be. That possessing and expressing a worldview and a code of moral behavior that are comfortably in conformance with what prevails in the respectable secular circles in which we live and work is no assurance of goodness and virtue. That Christ makes some special demands upon us that occasionally require us to be out of step. It is only if one has that sense of differentness—not animosity toward others in any sense, but differentness—that one has a chance of being strong enough to obey the teachings of Christ on many matters much more significant than Friday abstinence and Communion-fast rules—for example, rules of sexual morality.

The divergence of Christian teaching from the morality of the general society seems especially obvious (and especially blatant) today. Just turn on the tube any night, or walk up to any newsstand. But it would be wrong to think that this divergence between the ways of the world and Christian teaching is new. To the contrary, it is as old as the faith itself. And it sets that Christian apart not only from utterly decadent societies such as Sodom and Gomorrah, but even from purportedly moral societies, as Israel itself was when he was crucified. Christ said, "You will be hated by all men for my name's sake." He said at the Last Supper:

> If the world hates you, know that it has hated me before you. If you were of the world, the world would love what is its own. But because you are not of the world, but I have chosen you out of the world, therefore the world hates you.

And again:

> I have given them thy work; and the world has
> hated them, because they are not of the world,
> even as I am not of the world. I do not pray that
> thou take them out of the world, but that thou
> keep them from evil. They are not of the world,
> even as I am not of the world.

And he said to Pilate:

> My kingdom is not of this world. If my kingdom
> were of this world, my followers would have
> fought that I might not be delivered to the Jews.
> But, as it is, my kingdom is not from here.

That thought pervades the Gospels. It is also in the
early Church. Consider the following passage from a
letter of one of the early fathers in the late second century, describing the early Christians:

> Though residents at home in their own coun-
> tries, their behavior is more like that of tran-
> sients. They take their full part as citizens, but
> they also submit to everything as if they were
> aliens. For them, any foreign country is a home-
> land, and any homeland a foreign country.

And of course that same notion has come down
faithfully to modern Christianity. The most influential

devotional work, in English, in Protestant Christianity was called *The Pilgrim's Progress*, preserving the same ancient image of the Christian as an alien citizen, a traveler just passing through these parts on the way to the promised land.

It becomes quite obvious why the serious Christian must be a pilgrim, an alien citizen, a bit "different" from the world around him, when one considers how many Christian virtues make no sense whatever to the world. Consider, for example, the first and foremost Christian virtue, humility: awareness of the greatness of God and hence the insignificance of self. That is a crazy idea to the world, which values above all else self-esteem and self-assertion.

Or consider the Christian virtue (or practice) of self-denial. I am not talking about self-denial in the sense of refraining from what is sinful; but self-denial in the sense of deliberately depriving oneself of what is good and lawful, solely for the sake of doing penance and asserting the dominance of the spirit over the flesh. Self-denial in the sense of the serious fasting that the Gospels repeatedly describe Jesus as engaging in. Can the world possibly understand that? I had a teacher in high school, an elderly Jesuit, a saintly man, who was reputed to wear a hair shirt. My God, what a crazy thing! To wear this itchy thing just for the sake of being a little bit uncomfortable all day. It's almost—why, it's almost as crazy as John the Baptist. (I am not, let it be clear, recommending the hair shirt; personally, I can't even stand wearing synthetic blends. But my point is that only the Christian, and not the worldly person, can understand why one should not be deemed certifiably insane if he chooses to engage in such a practice.)

Or consider, finally, the Christian virtue of chastity. Except for divine command, it makes no sense. The world can find reasons for condemning dishonesty, deception, and manipulativeness in sexual relations. But if those secular evils are avoided—if the partners are really fond of each other, or are not *even* fond of each other, but both understand that they are just having a good time—what *possible* justification is there for chastity? Surely the worldly ideal is not chastity, but safe sex. And to preach the opposite is like—well, it's like talking about hair shirts.

When the values of Christ and of the world are so divergent—so inevitably divergent—we should not feel surprised if we find ourselves now and then "out of step." In fact, we should be worried if we are never that way. As Christ told us, we are *supposed* to be out of step. We must learn to accept it. Learn to take pride in it. For Jesus also said (and this is a scary thought):

> And I say to you, everyone who acknowledges me before men, him will the Son of Man also acknowledge before the angels of God. But whoever disowns me before men will be disowned before the angels of God.

I recently made remarks somewhat similar to these, at a father-daughter Communion breakfast at

Georgetown Visitation High School. The Gospel for the day—I guess it was the second Sunday of Advent—happened to fit in beautifully with the subject and gave me a new insight into how much Christ values our willingness to be different, to stand by his side against the world. It was the story of the Good Thief—Dismas, tradition tells us his name was. That story appears only in Luke, who sets the scene first as follows:

> And the people stood looking on; and the rulers with them kept sneering at him, saying, "He saved others; let him save himself, if he is the Christ, the chosen one of God." And the soldiers also mocked him, coming to him and offering him common wine, and saying, "If thou art the King of the Jews, save thyself!"

So here is Christ, lifted up on the cross, looking down over the crowd, dying, and what he sees and hears is nothing but rejection, repudiation, and mockery. Luke continues:

> Now one of those robbers who were hanged was abusing him, saying, "If thou art the Christ, save thyself and us!" But the other in answer rebuked him and said, "Dost not even thou fear God, seeing that thou art under the same sentence? And we indeed justly, for we are receiving what our deeds deserved; but this man has done nothing wrong." And he said to Jesus, "Lord, remember

> me when thou comest into thy kingdom." And
> Jesus said to him, "Amen I say to thee, this day
> thou shalt be with me in paradise."

What an extraordinary thing. Dismas is the *only* saint canonized by Christ Himself. The only human being, including even Mary, that we know *from the Gospels*, indeed from the mouth of Christ Himself, to be in heaven. So much did Jesus value that man's standing beside Him when all the world had abandoned Him. And the same reward, for the same willingness to go against the world, awaits us.

Christmas is coming up soon. The world will celebrate that with us. The world likes to celebrate. It has not observed with us, of course, the penitential season of Advent that precedes Christmas—a sort of mini-Lent, when Christians have traditionally deprived themselves. The world does not like to deprive itself. Perhaps, in observing faithfully what remains of Advent, we can recapture some sense of our distinctiveness, our positive "weirdness," as the world judges. What can be more incomprehensible to the world than *intentionally* depriving oneself of pleasure or satisfaction—*not* in order to lose weight, or to retain one's health, nor even because the pleasure is in any way sinful, but *solely* in order to mortify the flesh (as we used to say) and thereby to affirm commitment to the truth that our only lasting pleasure and satisfaction is not here, where we are alien citizens, but hereafter.

Moral Formation—the Character of Catholic Higher Education

Catholic institutions of higher learning were of particular importance to Justice Scalia, a graduate of Georgetown University. In this 1994 address at Catholic University, Scalia traced the history of religious colleges in the United States, arguing that their role has varied according to broader attitudes toward religion in society. The "secularization of our national character," in which the culture shows "no preference between religion and irreligion," means that Catholic schools face new obstacles and must operate accordingly to maintain their distinctive identity and unique purpose. And central to that purpose, "at least at the undergraduate level, must be precisely moral formation": a good Catholic school must teach students not only "to think well, but to live virtuously." Justice Scalia delivered this speech upon receiving a prestigious award from Catholic University.

I am genuinely honored to be a recipient of the Cardinal Gibbons Medal. Surely there are few awards in the country that have such a distinguished list of recipients—from John Kennedy to Nancy Reagan, and including, to mention a few of those I admire particularly, Fulton Oursler, Fulton J. Sheen, Cardinal Baum,

Archbishop Hannan, and Monsignor John Tracy Ellis.
I am proud to be in such company.

It is always somewhat intimidating to receive an
award from a Catholic organization. The Church has
been wise, I think, not to pronounce its greatest he-
roes, that is to say, its saints, until after they are
dead. Preferably not until long after they are dead,
so that their entire life can be considered with some
detachment—indeed, not merely with detachment but
with a devil's advocate to point out all the warts. In
honoring someone who may still go on to flub the dub,
you take some risk. I am relieved to observe, however,
that you are not honoring me for my saintliness; and
doubtless the choirs of angels are pleased with that as
well. Not to mention my loving but Hibernically frank
wife, Maureen.

Besides not honoring me for having achieved sanctification, I am sure you also do not honor me for my
position on what has become a defining issue for the
Catholic Church in America, and indeed throughout
the world: abortion. Or at least not for my position as
a federal judge regarding the constitutionality of laws
prohibiting that act. I accept no praise for that from
Catholics, but only from lawyers; because I would hold
otherwise, whatever my personal views on the practice, if I thought the law were different.

I am a natural object of your generosity, however,
because my ties to Catholic University, though perhaps not unusually close, have been unusually long.
I did my undergraduate studies, of course—in the

mid-1950s—not at Catholic but at Georgetown. I was well familiar with CU, however—partly because I used to travel with some frequency to Little Rome, that part of the city occupied by CU and many other Catholic institutions, including the usual object of my visits, Trinity College. Many was the evening I recall standing on the island across from Peoples Drug Store on Dupont Circle, waiting for the transfer bus that would take me up North Capitol Street to your part of the city.

I was also painfully familiar with Catholic University as the object of my intense envy because of its drama program. I was president of the Mask and Bauble Society during my time at Georgetown, and we did our best—though with little hope of success—to match the highly professional productions staged by the fabled Father Hartke, who, I may note, is another of my predecessors as recipient of the Cardinal Gibbons Medal. I think it is fair to say that, in those days of the '50s, we thespians at Georgetown had the same feelings toward the Catholic U theater group that the teams of the American League had toward the Damn Yankees. I am glad to see that the fine tradition of good theater at CU has held up better than the Yankees, and that Father Hartke was not succeeded by George Steinbrenner.

My later relations with CU were more sporadic. Of course I was reminded of it every year later in life—whether in Cambridge, Cleveland, Charlottesville, Washington, Chicago, or Palo Alto—as the annual church collection would be taken for its support. And

I would contribute or not, I must confess, depending upon whether one of its media theologians had rubbed me the wrong way that year. (That is one of the lesser reasons I am not up for sainthood.) During the 1970s I held, successively, several posts in the executive branch of the federal government. As one of them was coming to an end, I gave some thought to putting myself forward as a candidate for the deanship of your law school—and went so far as to interview with the search committee of the faculty. But I was wise enough, even at that young age, to conclude that being a law dean was indeed (as one of my former deans and mentors had described it) like running a zoo with the cages open. And since then, to bring my Catholic U career down to date, I have spoken several times at the university and at the law school, and have come to be a friend, if not a confidant, of Father Byron and Brother Ellis.

I am, ladies and gentlemen, not a proponent of after-dinner speeches, particularly heavy ones. And so I shall make my substantive remarks this evening quite brief. I want to say a few words about Catholic education, and about its place in modern America. What a Catholic university must be depends upon the society in which that university functions. In Europe in the Middle Ages, when everything around was Catholic, I suppose the task of a Catholic university was simply to be a university; to preserve, expand, and pass on the body of human knowledge. It had no special or peculiar responsibility, except perhaps in its schools of theology, for nurturing or keeping alive the faith, and the manner of life that the faith entails. With the Reformation, that changed, as the great universities of Europe, and later of America, divided themselves on denominational lines. I did my third year of study at Georgetown in its junior-year-abroad program at the University of Fribourg, which was the only Catholic university in Switzerland. The others, at Geneva and Lausanne, for example, were officially Protestant. And in this country, the earliest colleges and universities were also denominational.

Even so, however, after the Reformation and until the great upheaval of the Napoleonic Wars, Western society was still essentially Christian. It was still possible to speak of "Christendom." The sectarian universities, Catholic and Presbyterian, Lutheran, Congregationalist, Baptist and Methodist, espoused different dogmas, to be sure, but still taught, and existed in the midst of, a common, generally accepted Christian morality. That was true in the new United States no less than in Europe. While the magnificent Constitution we brought forth in 1787 banished sectarian religion from government, religion in general and Christianity in particular remained a prominent part of public life and manners. That lasted well into the nineteenth century, as the words to the "Battle Hymn of the Republic" well enough demonstrate.

That changed with the French Revolution, which ultimately spread throughout Europe a secularization of public life. The University of Paris, where Aquinas taught and Ignatius recruited Xavier to the Society of Jesus, became a secular state school. And that secularization eventually, though much later, came to these shores. Here it went through an intermediate stage, in which, acknowledging the identity and great contribution of our largest non-Christian religious minority, we became a nation that believed in, and celebrated, its Judeo-Christian character. That was not much of a stretch, after all, Christianity being—as the Romans recognized but we sometimes later forgot—a sect of Judaism. We were at that stage of development, the Judeo-Christian stage, when I was a boy—or at least we were at that stage in New York, where we acknowledged publicly our national beliefs in a personal God, and in certain common, revealed truths including the Decalogue, and agreed to differ respectfully about the rest.

One can trace the changes in America from the opinions of its Supreme Court—even (and indeed, especially) those opinions that were wrong about the law because they allowed it to be distorted by social beliefs. The prime example is one of my least favorite Supreme Court opinions, delivered without dissent in 1892, entitled *Church of the Holy Trinity v. United States*. The case involved a federal statute entitled "An Act to Prohibit the Importation and Migration of Foreigners and Aliens Under Contract or Agreement to Perform Labor in the United States, Its Territories, and the District of Columbia." A church in the city of New York made such a contract with an English minister, whereby he was to come to New York and serve as the church's rector and pastor, which he did. The United States sued the church for the penalty provided by the statute, and the trial court upheld the sanction. The Supreme Court reversed. Even though the language of the statute was categorical and made no exceptions for ministers (though it made exceptions for professional actors, artists, lecturers, and singers), the Court simply refused to read it to mean what it said. "It is a familiar rule," the Court said, "that a thing may be within the letter of the statute and yet not within the statute, because not within its spirit, nor within the intention of its makers." I do not believe that. I think the text enacted by Congress is the law, and the duty of the Court is to apply it (unless it be unconstitutional), rather than to consult spirits. That awful case is frequently cited to us by counsel who want us to ignore what the statute says. But for present purposes I am interested in another mistake the Court made. The spirits it listened to caused it to go on for eight pages leading to the following conclusion:

> These, and many other matters which might be noticed, add a volume of unofficial declarations to the mass of organic utterances that this is a Christian nation. In the face of all these, shall it be believed that a Congress of the United States intended to make it a misdemeanor for a church of this country to contract for the services of a Christian minister residing in another nation?

To be fair to the Court, its opinion made clear that it was just as unthinkable that the statute would prohibit a Jewish synagogue's importation of an "eminent rabbi." But the official recognition that we were a "Christian nation" surely had no place in the *United States Reports*. Legally it was false. But sociologically I have no doubt it was (in 1892) true—which is why the opinion was unanimous and so readily accepted.

For the next stage of our national development, the Judeo-Christian stage, we can jump forward about half a century in the *United States Reports*, to a case called *Zorach v. Clauson*, decided in 1952. It involved a program which I myself had been involved in in the New York City public schools—the so-called released-time program, in which public-school children of all faiths whose parents made the request could be released from school an hour early one day a week, to attend religious instruction or devotional exercises. New York City taxpayers challenged the practice as unconstitutional. The Court upheld it. The opinion for the Court by Justice Douglas, hardly one of the more conservative justices, spoke of Catholics, Protestants, and Jews, and included the following passage:

> We are a religious people whose institutions presuppose a Supreme Being. . . . When the state encourages religious instruction or cooperates with religious authorities by adjusting the schedule of public events to sectarian needs, it follows the best of our traditions. For it then

respects the religious nature of our people and
accommodates the public service to their spiritual needs.

That description of our national character reflects,
I think, stage two of our national sociological development: the Judeo-Christian stage, in which monotheistic religion in general was favored, though no
particular denomination.

The last and most recent stage, the secularization of
our national character, came quickly and is reflected
most clearly in the language of a 1968 Supreme Court
case called *Epperson v. Arkansas*. There you will find
no more talk about a "religious people," and about "accommodating the public service to [the people's] spiritual needs." "The First Amendment," the Court says
in *Epperson*, "mandates governmental neutrality"—
not merely between the various religious sects, but
"between religion and nonreligion."

My point in this discussion is not to criticize the
holdings of these cases, but to point out the progres-
sion that they demonstrate in the perception of our
national character: from a Christian nation, to a religious nation, to a nation that has no preference between religion and irreligion. I think that perception is
by and large accurate, at least insofar as concerns what
might be called the "governing classes" of society. The
signs of the passing of the old religiousness are everywhere. In our laws, for example, which now approve

many practices formerly forbidden because of a national aversion rooted primarily in religious beliefs. In our body of common knowledge, which used to include *The Pilgrim's Progress*, and now seemingly does not include the Bible. A recent survey found that only about half of the American people could name the first book of the Old Testament; only about a third could say who gave the Sermon on the Mount; and only about a fifth could name a single Old Testament prophet. A nation that used to abound with names like Ezekiel and Zebadiah now presumably thinks that the Beatitudes are a female singing group, and that the Apocrypha is a building in Greece. I read in a national newspaper recently a piece about some war-torn country, describing how anxious women went to church to "light a candle and make a prayer." "Make" a prayer! Our information media have begun to lose even the vocabulary of religion.

As one who believes in God, and who believes that those nations that love or at least fear Him, and do His will, will by and large prosper, I regret this secularization of our country, or at least of our intellectual classes. My object here, however, is not to bemoan or even criticize it, but to point out that it has a bearing upon what the nature and the mission of the modern American Catholic university must be. If you are serious about your Catholicism, you are operating in a more hostile environment, or at any rate in a less supportive environment, than used to be the case. That has several consequences which you must be prepared to accept—or else be prepared to lose your institutional soul.

First, you cannot expect to be as attractive a place for many faculty members and students as a secular institution that shares their beliefs and values (or the lack of them). If the place is indeed infused with Catholicism, it will be uncongenial. In the days when I was a law professor at the University of Chicago, I served for a term as a member of the Board of Visitors of the J. Reuben Clark Law School of Brigham Young University in Provo, Utah. Rex Lee, who is now the president of Brigham Young, and was then the dean of the law school, had been a colleague of mine at the Department of Justice. The J. Reuben Clark Law School was a place that had not lost its religious character— and for that reason would in some respects have been a difficult place for even me to teach. Oh, sure, it would have been sort of nice to stay in a place where dinner conversation does not stop and forks pause midway to the mouth when you mention that you have nine children. But I would have had to take on my entire daily ration of caffeine before I left home in the morning and would have had to sneak cigarettes in the men's room. In a Catholic university, there are, or ought to be, similar constraints concerning an expected lifestyle that is increasingly different from that of the surrounding world.

Indeed, I will go further than that. Part of the task of a Catholic university, at least at the undergraduate level, must be precisely moral formation. Not long ago, all colleges, even non-denominational ones, used to consider that their task: to teach young men and women (and college freshmen are indeed still young and impressionable) not merely to think well but to live virtuously. Perhaps because our society no longer has firm beliefs about what is virtuous, there are few if any non-denominational schools that even pretend to pursue that task—unless it is the service academies, which still seek to inculcate the values of honor, duty, and country. Catholic universities, however, cannot avoid that task, and indeed betray the expectations of tuition-paying Catholic parents if they shirk it. Demands for a moral and virtuous lifestyle that is different from much of the world about us will lose you faculty members; and it will lose you students. I think the alternative is to lose your Catholic character.

Besides constraints upon lifestyle, there are, yes, constraints upon what is taught. The only justification for a Catholic university, it seems to me, is that there is some distinctive approach to human knowledge that is peculiar to Catholic, or at least Christian, belief. Otherwise, devote the money to Newman Clubs on secular campuses, or give it to the missions. The existence of such a distinctive approach is no mirage. Georgetown University was a very Catholic place when I was there. One of the best lessons I learned was in the course of my oral comprehensive exam in my major subject, history, at the end of senior year. I had done pretty darned well during all of the questioning, and at the end my history professor, Dr. Wilkinson, to whom I am ever indebted, asked me one last, seemingly softball question: if I had to pick a single event as the most significant in all the history I had studied, what would it be? I say it was a softball question because there obviously could not be any single correct answer. So I groped for what might be a good one. What should I say? The Battle of Thermopylae? No, the Battle of Lepanto. No, the French Revolution. No, the Grand Convention of 1787. I forget what answer I gave, but it was wrong. The right one, Dr. Wilkinson informed me, was the Incarnation. Well, of course. Point taken, and an unforgettable lesson learned.

There are some things that must be taught at Catholic universities, and some things that must not: How to use human fetuses for useful scientific research, for example. Or how Mary was in fact not a virgin and Jesus had two brothers and a sister. Or how artificial birth control and abortion are morally okay. Is this a restriction on free intellectual inquiry? I think not. It is simply a restriction on where it shall be done and who shall pay. If one does not believe in such restrictions, one does not believe in Catholic dogma, and one should not believe in Catholic universities. Catholic universities do not exist, I suggest, simply to make it easier for the press to locate a Catholic theologian who disagrees with the Pope.

The American academic landscape is strewn with colleges and universities—many of them the finest, academically, in the land—that were once denominational but in principle or practice no longer are. Antioch University, for example, was founded by the Christian Church and was later Unitarian. Bucknell and the University of Chicago were Baptist. Dartmouth and Yale were Congregational. Duke, Northwestern, and Vanderbilt were Methodist. Lehigh was Episcopalian; Princeton, Presbyterian. I used to marvel, when I was a young man, at how institutions founded out of religious enthusiasm, and once imbued with religious zeal, could have so far changed. With foolish sectarian pride, I thought that could never happen to Catholic institutions. Of course I was wrong. We started later, but we are on the same road.

Catholic University has a heightened immunity against that development, because of its pontifical charter, because of its board of directors (the American bishops), and indeed because of its very name. But by the same token it has a heightened responsibility. To demand that any Catholic university be more Catholic than this school is to demand, so to speak, that it be more Catholic than the Pope. By and large the school has lived up to that responsibility. I do not mean to minimize the difficulty that entails—in reducing the size of the pool of brilliant faculty and students that the university can draw upon; in producing diminished esteem from a generally secularized national academic establishment; and in diverting financial and emotional resources toward difficult and unpleasant administrative tasks and even, sometimes, litigation. But as the parson says in *The Canterbury Tales*, if gold should rust, then what would iron do? All Catholic parents who aspire to send their children to Catholic universities—and not merely those who send them here—owe the directors, the administrators, and the faculty of this institution a debt of gratitude for the hard task they have undertaken.

St. Ignatius's Suscipe

———————

As a graduate of two Jesuit institutions—Xavier High School in New York City and Georgetown University—Justice Scalia had a special affinity for this prayer composed by St. Ignatius of Loyola, the founder of the Jesuit order.

Take, O Lord, and receive my entire liberty,
my memory, my understanding and my whole will.
All that I am and all that I possess You have
    given me:
I surrender it all to You to be disposed of
    according to Your will.
Give me only Your love and Your grace;
with these I will be rich enough, and will desire
    nothing more.

Away from the Noise— Making Retreats

How can people who believe in the transcendental maintain their religious principles? In this 1998 speech to a group of students from his alma mater, Georgetown University, Justice Scalia emphasized that religious retreats are particularly important opportunities to think through difficult problems "and, of course, to pray for guidance. . . . If you don't have a weekend to spare once a year to think exclusively about the things that really matter— well, you haven't planned your life correctly." Scalia also shared stories about some of the most formative experiences of his life and the lessons they taught him.

The little instruction sheet I got after I agreed to give this talk said that I should not talk about values in the abstract but should relate a few instances from my own life in which my values bore upon my decisions. I will do my best—though the fact is that I am not very good at such anecdotal discourse. I also detest the term *values*, which suggests to me a greater degree of interchangeability than ought to exist—as though the principles that guide a man's life are something like monetary exchange rates, subject to change with the times. (As in: "The value of the yen has fallen.") I prefer the view of things expressed by Sir Thomas More in the play *A Man for All Seasons*, when his friend the Duke of Norfolk urges him to sign the damned accession to the divorce, even if he doesn't really agree with it:

> Some men think the Earth is round, others think it flat; it is a matter capable of question. But if it is flat, will the King's command make it round? And if it is round, will the King's command flatten it? No, I will not sign.

You have just returned from a retreat. Any person who believes in the transcendental has to go on a retreat periodically. Because the world believes in the pragmatic rather than the transcendental, and you will lose your soul (that is to say, forget what and who you are) if you do not get away from the noise now and then to think about the First Things. In the Gospels, of course, Jesus is constantly going off all by himself; and he doubtless needed it less than we do.

The most memorable retreat of my life was the one that I made at the end of my senior year in high school—a Jesuit high school, St. Francis Xavier in New York. It was so memorable because it was the year in which the big decision had to be made: whether to go on to college or (as many of my classmates did) to go on to St. Andrew-on-Hudson, the Jesuit seminary for the New York Province. I might have made a heck of a Jesuit—though perhaps somewhat out of step these days. But I concluded I had certain talents that might do more good out in the world. And I am not referring exclusively to my capacity to procreate, though it is true that I have nine children. I was affected, I might add, by the fact that I was the end of my family—the only descendant of a previous generation that consisted of nine brothers and sisters. Anyway, a retreat was a good occasion to think that through; and, of course, to pray for guidance.

I somehow got out of the habit of making retreats. The world crept in—which is what those of us who do not enter the seminary or the convent (and perhaps many of those who do) have to worry about. I have gotten back into the habit in the last ten years, and I recommend it to you. If you don't have a weekend to spare once a year to think exclusively about the things that really matter—well, you haven't planned your life correctly.

Another thing I can tell you—with an anecdote or two to back it up—is that things do not work out the way you want, but the way God wants. And sometimes what seems to you a crushing disappointment may in fact be a great blessing. I won a Naval ROTC fellowship when I graduated from high school. It was very hard to get in those days. All I had to do to cash in on the fellowship was to be accepted at a college that had Naval ROTC. As it happened, the only college that did which I was interested in attending—very interested in attending—was Princeton. And Princeton turned me down. A major disappointment. So I came to Georgetown instead, and I am sure I am a different person (and a better person) than I would have been if *my* will had been done.

The next-biggest disappointment in my life was the morning in Palo Alto, California (I was teaching at Stanford Law School), when I received a phone call from the attorney general informing me that of the two finalists whom he had interviewed for the post of solicitor general, I had *not* been chosen. A really bad call on his part, I thought; and a bitter and unexpected disappointment for me. But had I become SG, I have little doubt that I would not be on the Supreme Court today. So pray for things, but accept what you are given; He knows better than you what is for your own good.

If you have transcendental principles—which for Catholics means if you believe in Jesus Christ and His Church—they have to shape your entire worldview. Perhaps the best lesson I ever learned here at Georgetown occurred during my oral comprehensive examination in my major (history) at the end of my senior year. My history professor was Dr. Wilkinson, a prince of a man. He was the chairman of the three-professor panel that examined me. And I did, if I may say so myself, a smashingly good job. As the time for the examination was almost at hand, Dr. Wilkinson asked me one last question, which seemed to me a softball. Of all the historical events you have studied, he said, which one in your opinion had the most impact upon the world? How could I possibly get this wrong? There was obviously no single correct answer. The only issue was what *good* answer I should choose. The French Revolution perhaps? Or the Battle of Thermopylae—or of Lepanto? Or the American Revolution? I forget what I picked, because it was all driven out of my mind when Dr. Wilkinson informed me of the *right* answer—or at least the right answer if I really believed what he and I thought I believed. Of course it was the Incarnation. Point taken. You must keep everything in perspective, and not run your spiritual life and your worldly life as though they are two separate operations.

And finally I want to tell you something my father told me that I have never forgotten. You are all here at Georgetown, devoted to the life of the mind, admiring your brilliant professors and envying, perhaps, your brilliant classmates. My father was also committed to the life of the mind—much more of an intellectual than I ever was or can be. He taught Romance languages at Brooklyn College, and of course once you have mastered the grammar of a language there is nothing to do but read all the great literature and philosophy that has been written in that language. Which is what my father did. As my mother described it, he always had a book in front of his face. So this was not a man who spurned the life of the mind. But on one occasion he told me this (I have never forgotten it, and if you take away nothing else from this talk, I hope this will be it): "Son, brains are like muscles. You can rent them by the hour. The only thing that is not for sale is character."

Keep things in perspective, including the value of this education you are getting. At the end of the day, it is not that which will make you a good or a bad person.

The Indispensability of Courage—Military Service and the Christian

---

What habits are conducive to the practice of Christian virtues, and how does one develop them? Justice Scalia's high school— Xavier High School in Manhattan—is a Jesuit institution with a military regiment. When he returned there to speak in 2011, the justice reflected on what he called the "union between faith and service." Justice Scalia argued that because military service helps form the necessary habit of courage, it "is not only appropriate for Christians, it is conducive to Christian virtue."

Men of Xavier: Many thanks for your warm and generous welcome. It is my great pleasure to be with you this evening to celebrate the Regiment and to recognize the achievements of those being honored with awards. The Regiment, as I remember it, is a place where awards are earned; so I have no doubt you and your families are deservedly proud of what you have accomplished. Congratulations.

Whatever regimental glory I won when I graduated in 1953 is unrecorded. The one distinctively military item I recall is that I rose to the rank of lieutenant colonel, commanding officer of the marching band. I count that an honor because traditionally the post had been held by a major. Xavier's official history—published in 1997 on the occasion of the school's 150th birthday—notes only one achievement of mine: while an underclassman, I represented Xavier on a panel of students from schools throughout the city on a Sunday-morning television show called *Mind Your Manners*. It was reported afterward that my "keen sensible answers, well seasoned with a bit of humor, stole the show." I think that may have been the peak of my favorable press coverage.

My talk this evening is about the legacy to which you and I are heirs. Xavier High School was the most formative institution in my life; and as I look back on those times, fifty-eight years later, it is the Regiment I remember most. Then as now, military training was the distinctive tradition that set Xavier apart (and Xavier men apart) from the other Jesuit schools in the city—a link to the broader tradition of American military academies. And situated in New York, in the heart of American Catholicism, the Regiment has also been a visible sign of the patriotism of the Catholic citizens of this country.

Xavier's contribution to the armed forces began even before it became a military school. At the outset of the Civil War, about half the population of the city was made up of Catholics; and in those days, to put it mildly, Catholics were not universally beloved, or even trusted, by their Protestant brethren. Military service on behalf of the Union did much to dispel that mistrust. In 1861, eight regiments of predominantly Catholic New Yorkers volunteered to fight for the Union. Many of them were Irish—no surprise there, since the Irish national anthem begins, "Soldiers are we."

Although Xavier was small and young then, she sent a number of her sons to the Union Army, including James Rowan O'Beirne, who won the Medal of Honor for holding a line under withering enemy fire, and later, as provost marshal of Washington, led the manhunt for Lincoln's assassins.

Xavier also sent three of her priests to serve as chaplains. One of them, Father Michael Nash, had been a prefect at Xavier, and evidently a strict one. Father Nash was assigned to minister to a famously rough company of volunteers called Wilson's Zouaves. When they first met Father Nash, Wilson's Zouaves had less interest in confession than they did in drinking and brawling. But Father Nash stuck it out, and by the time the whole company had sailed to Florida, where they were to serve, they carried him ashore on their shoulders. According to an 1897 history of Xavier, thanks to Father Nash the Zouaves "proved to be true patriots, obedient and brave, a bulwark of the country, the terror of the enemy." If that seems to you a bit much to attribute to a chaplain, you should know the aforementioned history was written by the Alumni Association. But whatever its motivations, the account properly recognizes that the military service of Xavier's priests was in the best tradition of the Church and the Society of Jesus. It says:

> Called from the professor's chair to bear all the hardships of military life, they showed again and again that the sons of the knightly Loyola have inherited the undaunted soul of their founder. . . . By their faithful work as Christian priests they infused into their men greater and nobler and purer patriotism. On the field of battle, scorning fear and danger, they sought the wounded and dying amidst flying bullets, and were good Samaritans alike to Catholic and non-Catholic, to friend and foe.

A few decades later, Xavier's military tradition began in earnest. By the 1890s, Xavier would become "the Catholic military school." Military training became compulsory for all students; and the Regiment became the public image of the school in New York. Captain John Drum, an army officer who would later give his life on San Juan Hill, organized students into separate companies and taught them military drill. A fife-and-bugle corps was established, and Xavier's cadets began to assume a place of honor in New York City parades on public holidays like St. Patrick's Day, Decoration Day (what we now call Memorial Day), and Columbus Day. Those honors culminated in 1897, Xavier's golden-jubilee year, when the corps of cadets was invited to participate in the dedication of Grant's

Tomb. An account written that year records that "[t]he department of Military Science has become more and more a part of the life of the College."

I have no doubt those first Xavier cadets played a small but important role in reinforcing public perceptions of Catholic loyalty and civic virtue. The need for such reinforcement should not be underestimated. In the late nineteenth century, religious hostilities were real and deep. In 1884, Republican presidential candidate James G. Blaine came to New York to attend a morning meeting. Blaine looked good to win the election, which was just days away. But on that fated morning, a Presbyterian minister named Samuel Burchard rose to give a speech supporting Blaine. Burchard assailed the Democrats as "the party whose antecedents have been rum, Romanism, and rebellion." Blaine failed to rebuke Burchard, and Irish Catholics in this city, as you may imagine, did not care for that a'tall a'tall. They turned out in droves and defeated Blaine in New York by just over one thousand votes— costing him the election.

That was the era when Xavier's students began to put on the cadet's uniform, and I think it improved the public's perception of Catholics. For once, the *New York Times* agrees that I am right—even if you have to go back to May 31, 1894, to read about it. The *Times* published a rebuke of an anti-Catholic organization called the American Protective Association and its leader, the Reverend Madison C. Peters. The APA and Peters accused Catholics of "Romanizing the army and navy" and proposed to prevent them from holding public office or command positions in the armed forces, on the grounds (I suppose) that if given a battalion to command, a Catholic colonel might turn the unit over to the Pope. To its credit the *Times* published a piece entitled "Object Lesson for Bigots: Catholic and Protestant in the Memorial Parade." The article reminded the reader that the previous day New York had hosted a parade for the Grand Army of the Republic—a procession of veterans of the Civil War. The procession comprised "men of all creeds and nationalities who had followed the Stars and Stripes together in many a hard fight regardless whether the men in front of them or behind them were Roman Catholics or Protestants, Jews or Gentiles." The article described a memorial service that had been held that day in the Church of St. Francis Xavier, at which "the students of [the college], to the number of 300," who had been "under the instruction and drill of Capt. Drum of the United States Army," "appeared in full military costume in honor of the occasion." The *Times* continued:

> It is instructive to turn from these terrible and distorted pictures of the Roman Catholics and their Church, as Mr. Peters draws them, to the reality as witnessed yesterday at St. Francis Xavier's. . . . The great edifice was crowded to the doors with devout worshippers, who were privileged to listen to a sermon that was as full

of glowing, broad-minded patriotism as are the sermons of Mr. Peters full of prejudice and bigotry.

That sermon was delivered right here, in this church. It reminded those present that obedience to lawful authority is the religious duty of every Catholic, and that Catholics had proved their loyalty on the battlefield.

It is easy for us, more than a century later, to take for granted that no serious person seriously doubts the patriotism of his Catholic neighbors—though the ugly old slanders do occasionally rear their heads. But we should not forget the small debt we owe to the members of this Regiment who were willing to become conspicuous examples of Catholics living their faith by serving their country. Probably the most striking symbol of that union between faith and service was the military Mass. One historian reports that by the end of the nineteenth century (and partly as a protest against the Reverend Peters and his APA), Xavier began holding special military Masses to open the month of May and its special devotions to Mary. At that Mass, "the cadets processed into church and the officers sat in the front pews with their swords unsheathed—imitating the crusading knights of the past—during the reading of the Gospel and the profession of the Creed. A trumpet sounded during the Consecration of the bread and wine." It was ceremonial flair with a purpose. The tradition was still alive during my days here. On First

Fridays the regiment would attend morning Mass in dress blues (dress blues were the uniform of the day on Fridays). Just before the consecration, the regimental officers would march down the center aisle in a column of twos, swords drawn and resting on their right shoulders; the front of the column would divide left and right at the altar rail, producing a single line across the transepts and forming, with the officers remaining in the main aisle, a cross of regimental blue. The elevation of the Host would be announced by a bugle's flourishes instead of a bell, and the officers, from front to rear, would present swords.

By the 1930s, the Regiment had become a part of the pageantry of the city. In 1932, New York held the biggest parade since World War I to celebrate the bicentennial of George Washington's birthday. Xavier was the only high school unit to participate—a great honor. The entire Regiment assembled for the parade, stretched out for three or four blocks east of Fifth Avenue. They did draw dreary duty, however: they marched last, so they were stuck where they stood from morning until late afternoon. The whole regiment continued to march in major New York parades during my days here—and its place in the pageant had improved considerably. We used to march right behind the first military unit in the parade, the Fighting 69th, New York City's regiment. I will never forget participating in what I have been told was the last real ticker-tape parade, before the ticker-tape machine became technologically obsolete: the parade celebrating General Douglas MacArthur's return from Japan.

Over the years, it became commonplace to see Xavier cadets in their ROTC uniforms, or in dress blues on Fridays, on the subways from four boroughs (Staten Islanders took the ferry), on the trains from New Jersey, and even from as far up the Hudson as Verplanck, New York (one of my classmates was from there). I was a member of the JV rifle team, so I occasionally had to bring my .22 carbine on the subway from Queens to school, or to the gunsmith in Brooklyn. (Imagine that today.) Periodically, on the occasion of major liturgical celebrations, the police would stop traffic on 16th Street while the whole Regiment marched, to the music of the band and the drum-and-bugle corps, down the impressive front steps of the school, column left along 16th Street, and column left again into the Church of St. Francis Xavier for Mass; and afterward we would parade back—all in dress blues.

But the Regiment's most important legacy, of course, was not pageantry; it was discipline, and duty, and sacrifice. Nearly a thousand of Xavier's sons served in the First World War—including Captain Drum's son, Hugh, a Xavier man who eventually rose to the rank of lieutenant general. World War II saw nearly fifteen hundred Xavier men fight for their country, fifty-four of whom gave their lives. Like Father Nash in the Civil War, ten Jesuit teachers and nine lay faculty left the school to serve. Historian Helen McNulty writes that

Xavier was "one of the few high schools in the country which had thoroughly prepared students to participate in modern military warfare. . . . It is believed that no high school in the United States made a greater contribution in manpower and effort during WWII than Xavier High School." I believe it. And at a military Mass in 1947, with the war over, Cardinal Spellman—who was archbishop of both New York and the United States military—read aloud Pope Pius XII's handwritten letter to Xavier's president, Father Tynan, offering the Holy Father's "prayerful remembrance . . . of those whose courage and self-sacrifices made the proud present possible."

But as you know, the tradition of Xavier as a thoroughly military academy did not survive the antimilitary sentiment of the Vietnam War. I lamented when the school announced that the Regiment would no longer be compulsory, and I continue to think that was a mistake. This country has a rich tradition of military schools. It was born partly of necessity—since with independence from Britain came the need to have an army and to run it competently—but it was also born partly of democratic theory. Congress first authorized the creation of the United States Military Academy at West Point in 1802. But that academy, of course, could not educate the whole country in military matters—and in those days, the whole country might well be called upon to serve as militia. Following the War of 1812, the Committee on Militia of the House of Representatives reported to Congress its belief that

the safety of a republic depends as much upon
the equality in the use of arms amongst its citizens, as upon the equality of rights; nothing can
be more dangerous in such a government than
to have a knowledge of the military art confined
to a part of the people—for sooner or later that
part will govern.

Military schools followed different paths in the
North and South. In the South, it became common
for states to establish and fund public military academies. Two of them—the Virginia Military Institute
and South Carolina's Citadel—were resurrected after
the Civil War and continue an illustrious tradition. But
in the North, states took a more laissez-faire approach.
Private military schools sprang up, including many run
by religious denominations. Xavier was one of a number of Catholic military secondary schools established
in the nineteenth century—including LaSalle Military
Academy on Long Island, and Canisius College (Jesuit, of course) in Buffalo. All Hallows College in Utah
was a military school, and Catholic universities, such
as Notre Dame and St. Louis University (Jesuit), had
compulsory military training. It was, as I have said,
part of the long connection between Catholics and the
armed forces. West Point has had a disproportionate
share of Roman Catholics, enough to justify a separate
chapel since 1899.

Xavier has been a prominent part of that Catholic tradition. Catholicism, of course, has never had

that contempt for the soldier that came to the fore in Vietnam-era America. The Roman centurion at the Crucifixion who said, "Truly this was the son of God," was not one of the bad guys. Nor the centurion who asked Jesus to heal his servant without the necessity of going there (the famous line, echoed at Mass, "Lord, I am not worthy that you should enter under my roof, but only say the word and my servant will be healed"). Of him, Jesus said he had not seen such faith in Israel. And while Jesus said that he who lives by the sword will die by the sword, He did not regard soldiers as men who lived by the sword. His advice to them was not "Throw down your arms," but "Be content with your wages." (The real villains in the Gospels, I am sorry to say, were the lawyers—though to be fair they were lawyers in a theocratic state, so that their closest modern equivalent is probably, imagine that!, theologians.) Two of the earliest and most venerated of Christian martyrs, St. Sebastian and St. George, were soldiers of Diocletian. And come to think of it, Ignatius Loyola— "the knightly Loyola," as the Alumni Association puff piece I quoted earlier described him—was a soldier. And his successors are still called generals.

The defining virtue of a soldier is courage. What chastity is to a nun, or humility to a friar, courage is to a soldier. In *The Screwtape Letters*, C. S. Lewis imagines a senior demon, Screwtape, sending advice to his nephew Wormwood on how to ensnare the soul of an Englishman living on the brink of World War II.

Screwtape tells Wormwood that the demons have managed to fool mankind into believing that many virtues are vices—that modesty is prudishness, for example. But that has not worked for the virtue of courage.

> We have made men proud of most vices, but not of cowardice. Whenever we have almost succeeded in doing so, the Enemy [that is, God] permits a war or an earthquake or some other calamity, and at once courage becomes so obviously lovely and important even in human eyes that all our work is undone, and there is still at least one vice of which they feel genuine shame.

I believe that military service is not only appropriate for Christians, it is conducive to Christian virtue. I know of no other profession where one *commits* to laying down his life for his friends. I have nine children, whom I have sent to many different colleges, including two Jesuit colleges. I can say in all honesty that the school which took most seriously, which made a large part of each day's *instruction*, the task of *moral formation*—of developing character, and instilling fidelity to duty, honor, country—was West Point. And training oneself to be a soldier, preparing oneself to make that sacrifice if needed, is not just one more interchangeable way for a Christian to develop good character. Let no one demean it. It is good training indeed.

Let me leave you with this illustration: There was a Xavier man in the class above me named Donald Cook. On New Year's Eve, 1964, Marine Captain Donald Cook was taken prisoner by the Viet Cong—and remained their prisoner until his death. For his conduct as a prisoner of war, Cook was posthumously promoted to colonel and awarded the Medal of Honor. His citation for conspicuous gallantry reads in part:

> Despite the fact that by doing so he would bring about harsher treatment for himself, [Cook] established himself as the senior prisoner, even though in actuality he was not. Repeatedly assuming more than his share of [responsibility for] their health, Colonel Cook willingly and unselfishly put the interests of his comrades before that of his own well-being and, eventually, his life. Giving more needy men his medicine and drug allowance while constantly nursing them, he risked infection from contagious diseases while in a rapidly deteriorating state of health. This unselfish and exemplary conduct, coupled with his refusal to stray even the slightest from the Code of Conduct, earned him the deepest respect from not only his fellow prisoners, but his captors as well. Rather than negotiate for his own release or better treatment, he steadfastly frustrated attempts by the Viet Cong to break his indomitable spirit and passed this same re-

solve on to the men with whose well-being he so closely associated himself. Knowing his refusals would prevent his release prior to the end of the war, and also knowing his chances for prolonged survival would be small in the event of continued refusal, he chose nevertheless to adhere to a Code of Conduct far above that which could be expected. His personal valor and exceptional spirit of loyalty in the face of almost certain death reflected the highest credit upon Colonel Cook, the Marine Corps, and the United States Naval Service.

It also reflected great credit on the Regiment. To return to C. S. Lewis (I can't resist): Screwtape warns Wormwood that a war can be dangerous for their satanic cause, because it awakens men from their moral stupor. He says:

> This, indeed, is probably one of the Enemy's motives for creating a dangerous world—a world in which moral issues really come to the point. He sees as well as you do that courage is not simply *one* of the virtues, but the form of every virtue at the testing point, which means, at the point of highest reality. A chastity or honesty, or mercy, which yields to danger will be chaste or honest or merciful only on conditions. Pilate was merciful till it became risky.

The indispensability of courage is easier for the soldier to appreciate, whose very life may depend upon the courage of his comrades. Its value is harder to appreciate in the layman's endless days of peace, where the type of courage that is called for is rarely the physical courage to risk one's life. But for most of us, that is the long fight we are in for—courageously setting things right in the world God has created, starting with ourselves. The habit of courage is not acquired by study; it is forged by practice. And there is no better practice than the Regiment. By demanding obedience to duty, manly honor and discipline, frank and forthright acknowledgment of error, respect for ranks above and solicitude for ranks below, assumption of responsibility including the responsibility of command, willingness to sacrifice for the good of the corps—by demanding all those difficult things the Regiment develops *moral courage*, which, in the Last Accounting we must give, is the kind that matters. That is why military training is not, and never will be, just one more interchangeable way for young Christians to develop good character or learn to serve others. It is one of the noblest ways, and never let anyone tell you otherwise.

Faith and Work—How Belief Affects Vocation

Although Justice Scalia often encouraged Christians to apply their faith in their everyday lives, he recognized that how to live out one's vocation "depends primarily upon what one's vocation is." As he explained in this 1992 speech, his vocation as a judge barred him from indulging his Catholic beliefs from the bench. He ruled as he did on cases about abortion, for example, not because of his Catholic beliefs, but because of his legal philosophy. There is no Catholic way of being a judge, he explains, just as there is no Catholic way to make a hamburger, except to do it "honestly and perfectly."

I am happy to join you this evening in celebration of the thirtieth anniversary of the *Long Island Catholic*. I am an appropriate speaker for the occasion, I suppose, since I am myself a Long Island Catholic. I grew up in Elmhurst, and as a child used to spend the major part of my vacations at a little summer cottage my grandfather had built a stone's throw from here—in the days when Woodbury was still the country. At that time, of course, the *Long Island Catholic* did not exist; our paper was the *Brooklyn Tablet*. It is always good to come back.

When Monsignor Maniscalco invited me to give this talk, he specified the subject that you have printed on the program before you—"Personal Conscience, Public Person"—but he described at some greater length just what he meant that subject to embrace. I quote from his letter:

> How one's faith and one's judicial obligations either reinforce one another or create a degree of tension or both; whether, indeed, someone who holds high office in a pluralistic society is able to fulfill the Church's vision of the laity bringing Christian values to the world of which they are a part.

I always try to stick fairly closely to the text I have been assigned. This is a tricky one, but I will give it a try.

How one's faith affects the practice of one's vocation depends primarily upon what one's vocation is. No matter how good a Catholic a short-order chef may be, for example, there is no such thing as a Catholic hamburger. Unless, of course, it is a perfectly made and perfectly cooked hamburger. That is, I suppose, one way in which the faith affects all vocations: when Christ said, "Be ye perfect, as your heavenly Father is perfect," I think he meant perfect in all things, including that very important thing, the practice of one's lifework. A good Catholic cannot be an intentionally sloppy worker—or to the extent that he is a sloppy worker, he is a less satisfactory Catholic. Jesus of Nazareth the twenty-nine-year-old carpenter had never put together a poorly made cabinet. *Laborare est orare*, the old monastic motto goes. To work is to pray. And to work badly is to pray badly.

But beyond this aspect of Catholic belief that affects *all* professions and occupations, how and whether one's faith affects one's work depends entirely upon what one's work happens to be. In some occupations, certain connections are clear: A Catholic doctor cannot, consistent with his faith, perform an abortion or assist a suicide. A Catholic publisher cannot, consistent with his faith, market obscenity, libel, or pornography. But what about the area of "public life"—that is, the profession of government service—which is my assigned topic for this evening?

Let me talk first about the legislative and executive branches—I will discuss judges last. There are those who believe that it is wrong for an executive or a legislative official to pursue a policy that he deems desirable solely because of his religious beliefs. Indeed, there is at least one Supreme Court opinion suggesting that legislative action which is religiously motivated is unconstitutional. That seems to me quite wrong. The Free Exercise Clause of the First Amendment is violated when legislative or executive action is directed against others' religious beliefs; but neither the Free Exercise Clause nor the Establishment Clause is violated simply because legislative or executive action pursues a policy that the lawmaker or executive considers desirable because of his own religious belief. It would be quite impossible to apply such a principle. The religious person—the truly religious person—

cannot divide all of his policy preferences into those
that are theologically motivated and those that proceed from purely naturalistic inclinations. Can any of
us say whether he would be the sort of moral creature
he is without a belief in a Supreme Lawgiver, and hence
in a Supreme Law? I am reminded of G. K. Chesterton's
humorous poem entitled "The Song of the Strange As-
cetic," in which the narrator describes the sort of self-
indulgent, lustful, power-seeking life he would lead if
he were a heathen—ending each stanza, however, with
the observation that Higgins is a heathen, and Higgins
does none of those things! Higgins is a Scrooge-like,
nose-to-the-grindstone, abstemious, teetotaling, utterly dull banker. The poem ends:

> Now who that runs can read it,
> The riddle that I write,
> Of why this poor old sinner
> Should sin without delight—
> But I, I cannot read it
> (Although I run and run),
> Of them that do not have the faith,
> And will not have the fun.

Besides the practical impossibility of distinguishing
all religiously motivated social policies from those that
would exist even without religious motivation, adopting the principle that religiously motivated government
policies are un-American would require the rewriting
of a good deal of American history. The primary impetus for the drive to abolish slavery was a religious one.

Recall the words of the "Battle Hymn of the Republic," which ends, "As He died to make men holy, let us die to make men free, While God is marching on." The same is true of government laws prohibiting the manufacture and sale of strong drink, up to and including the constitutional amendment instituting Prohibition: mandated temperance was a religious cause. Religious motivation underlies many traditional laws still on the books, such as those against bigamy, or those proscribing public nudity. Societies with different religious beliefs manage well enough without them. Far from being a nation that has excluded religious-based policies from the sphere of government, official public expression of belief in God, and the adoption of policies thought by the people to be in accord with God's law, have distinguished us from most Western democracies, at least in the current century.

Of course, to acknowledge that religiously based social policies are not *ipso facto* unconstitutional is not to affirm the opposite: that they are *ipso facto* constitutional (though there is no question, I think, of the constitutionality of laws regulating traditional areas of public morality—laws preserving *bonos mores*, to use the common-law expression). Moreover, to say that a religiously motivated law would be constitutional is not to say that it would necessarily be wise. Laws severely restricting civil divorce, for example, are constitutional, but surely it is a matter of prudence whether they will achieve more good than harm in a society with a large plurality that no longer shares the moral premises on which they were based. Of course at some point the moral imperatives are so overwhelming that there is no room for prudential compromise. One does not argue about whether it will do more harm than good to oppose laws permitting genocide. That is in essence the Church's position regarding laws permitting abortion.

Mentioning the Big A (that is what the abortion issue is called on Capitol Hill) leads me quite naturally into the next part of this talk. Up until now I have been speaking about the relationship between religious belief and "public life" insofar as the legislative and executive branches are concerned. You will recall that I said at the outset, however, that how one's faith affects one's work depends upon what one's work happens to be. The work of the judicial branch is fundamentally different from that of the legislative and executive—or at least it is fundamentally different as I view things. Unlike presidents, cabinet secretaries, senators, and representatives, federal judges do not (or are not supposed to) *make* policy, but rather are to discern accurately and apply honestly the policies adopted by the people's representatives in the text of statutes—except to the extent that those statutes conflict with the text, the underlying traditions, or valid Supreme Court interpretation of the United States Constitution. Just as there is no Catholic way to cook a hamburger, so also there is no Catholic way to interpret a text, analyze a historical tradition, or discern the meaning and legitimacy of prior judicial decisions—except, of course, to do those things *honestly* and *perfectly*.

I find myself somewhat embarrassed, therefore, when Catholics, or other opponents of abortion, come forward to thank me earnestly for my position concerning *Roe v. Wade*. I must tell them that I deserve no thanks; that that position is not a virtuous affirmation of my religious belief, or even a sagacious policy choice, but simply the product of lawyerly analysis of constitutional text and tradition; and that if legal analysis had produced the opposite conclusion I would have come out the other way, regardless of their or my views concerning abortion. My religious faith can give me a personal view on the right or wrong of abortion; but it cannot make a text say yes where it in fact says no, or a tradition say "we permit" where it in fact has said "we forbid." If my position on *Roe v. Wade* were a reflection of Catholic beliefs and policy preferences, then I would say that the Constitution not only *permits* the banning of abortion, but *requires* it. Imaginative judges have derived results much more implausible than that from the provision of the Constitution that says no person shall be deprived of life, liberty, or property without due process of law. In fact, however, the Constitution does not *ban* abortion any more than it confers a right to abortion, and no amount of religious faith or zealous enthusiasm can change that.

These remarks reflect, of course, a view of the Constitution as a document containing a fixed and limited number of specific guarantees that do not expand and contract from age to age (though of course they must be applied to new phenomena). That is the traditional view. In recent years, however, the American people seem to have become persuaded that the Constitution is not a fixed and limited text, but rather an all-purpose, shorthand embodiment of *whatever they care deeply about.* Do we abhor the burning of the flag? Why, then, it must be constitutional to criminalize it. Do we favor homosexual rights? Why, then, it *must* be unconstitutional to deny them. And so forth, through a whole list of passionately felt issues, down to and including both sides of the abortion issue. Never mind the constitutional text; never mind the tradition that underlies that text. We know what we want, and if we want it passionately enough, it must be guaranteed (or if we hate it passionately enough, it must be prohibited) by the Constitution! We cannot leave such issues to be decided by the democratic process; only *un*important issues belong there. The really significant, heartfelt issues are *all* resolved in the Constitution, whether the text says anything about them or not. And we will ensure that the Constitution means what we want it to mean by interrogating nominees to the Supreme Court concerning all the "unenumerated" rights that we care about, one after another—conducting a plebiscite on the Constitution, in effect, each time a new nominee is put forward.

How different this is from the traditional American notion of what the Constitution means—from the notion that prevailed until very recently—is evident from considering the Nineteenth Amendment, adopted in 1920, which provides that "[t]he right of citizens of the United States to vote shall not be denied or abridged by the United States or by any State on account of sex." No one doubted that a constitutional amendment was necessary for that purpose, even though, in 1920 as today, the Constitution forbade denial of "equal protection of the laws." What could be more obviously a denial of equal protection than denial of the vote? But the Americans of 1920 understood, as the Americans of 1992 seemingly do not, that the vague provisions of the Constitution, such as the Equal Protection Clause and the Due Process Clause, are not invitations to constitutionalize our current desires from age to age, but rather bear a constant meaning that accords with the understanding of those terms when they were adopted. Standing by itself, the phrase "equal protection" can mean almost anything. As applied to distinctions between the sexes, it *could* be thought to require unisex public toilets and dormitories. Of course it does not mean that, because no one ever thought it meant that. So also (the Americans of 1920 understood) with respect to the right to vote.

The problem with making the Constitution an all-purpose embodiment of our current preferences—pro-abortion, anti-abortion, or anything else—is that it deprives the Constitution of its essential character as an *obstacle* to majority self-will and converts it (ironically) into a mechanism for placing the majority's current will beyond further democratic debate. The danger of that development—and the consequent need to restrain yourselves from asserting that all your deeply held beliefs are constitutional imperatives—is the only moral I hope to leave you with this evening. It is a moral rooted in law rather than theology, so if you have awarded me for my theological skill, you have been greatly deceived.

Really Present

BY PATRICK J. SCHILTZ

I talked to (then) Judge Scalia for the first time in the fall of 1983, when I interviewed for a clerkship with him. We talked about our shared Catholic faith—and, in particular, about the impact of his faith on his work as a federal judge. I talked to Justice Scalia for the last time in the fall of 2015, when he came to Minneapolis to speak at the University of Minnesota and the University of St. Thomas. We talked again about our faith—this time about the impact of my faith on my work as a federal judge. In the intervening thirty-three years, we had countless conversations, and there were few of them that did not touch in some way on faith.

That was to be expected. After my clerkship ended, our conversations were more about life than about law, and to talk to Justice Scalia about life was to talk to him about faith. His faith was his lodestar. The center of Justice Scalia's life as a Catholic—and thus the center of his life—was the Eucharist. I first attended Mass with Justice Scalia in early 1986, during the first of my two years clerking for him. His mother died just before Christmas in 1985, and his father died about two weeks later. My co-clerks and I had a Mass offered for them at Holy Rosary Church in Washington, D.C. Holy Rosary was just a few blocks from the courthouse, and it had been founded by Italian immigrants. The memorial Mass for Justice Scalia's parents was celebrated at noon on a weekday in January or February. Only a handful of people attended.

Catholics believe that when the bread and wine are consecrated during the Eucharistic Prayer in the Mass, they are transformed into the Body and Blood of Christ—the actual, not merely symbolic, Body and Blood of Christ. This belief—known as the doctrine of transubstantiation—is one of the most difficult doctrines for non-Catholics to understand. But Justice Scalia left no doubt about the sincerity of his belief.

What sticks in my mind about that first Mass with Justice Scalia was the intensity with which he worshipped—and, in particular, the intensity with which he prayed during the Eucharistic Prayer. Kneeling, head bowed, eyes closed, hands tightly clasped, brow deeply furrowed, Justice Scalia was so focused that he almost seemed to be in pain. But at the moment of the consecration of the bread—and then again at the moment of the consecration of the wine—he would raise his head, open his eyes, and look intently at the newly consecrated bread or wine as the priest held it aloft.

The fact that I can still remember this over thirty years later testifies to its impact on me. I grew up in the immediate aftermath of Vatican II, when the Church was struggling to figure out how it would pass on the faith to children. There was a sense that catechists should not dwell on the "old stuff"—such as the doctrine of transubstantiation—but no sense about what should replace it. And thus, while I grew up aware of the doctrine, I cannot really say that I internalized it. When I was at Mass, I would often be unengaged, and my attention would often wander.

That changed after I worshipped with Justice Scalia in that empty church on that cold day in 1986. Kneeling next to him, I realized that this was what it looked like when someone truly believed what I professed to believe. If I truly believed that Jesus Christ was present, I should be praying with intensity, not thinking about where to go for lunch. And if I truly believed that Jesus Christ was present fifty feet in front of me under the appearance of bread and wine, I should be looking at him, not at the bad toupee of the man in the next pew.

After attending one Mass with Justice Scalia, I never worshipped—or thought about worship—the same way.

Patrick J. Schiltz has served as a federal district judge in Minnesota since 2006. He was a law clerk to then–D.C. Circuit judge Scalia from 1985 to 1986 and again to Justice Scalia during the justice's first year on the Court, its October 1986 term.

Confessing the Faith

BY A. GREGORY GRIMSAL

In September 2015, I was a guest of Justice and Mrs. Scalia at their home on the Outer Banks of North Carolina for what they called "Beach Week," their annual retreat before October term. Although Justice Scalia not infrequently did some work at the beach, the general order of business inclined to good food, good wine, and good humor. In the evening, after dinner, out on the deck, the gentlemen smoked cigars, watched the stars, and identified but not always solved the world's problems.

On the last night of my visit, our little group went to a restaurant to celebrate the Scalias' wedding anniversary. Over cocktails, Justice Scalia produced a pair of showstopper earrings for Mrs. Scalia. It was a large and vinous evening. Once we returned to the house, Justice Scalia slipped up to his little crow's nest of an office, while everybody else faded quickly and, one by one, went off to bed. As it happened, I was left alone in the living room, hoping to finish reading a chapter in the book I'd brought before I, too, faded.

Presently, Justice Scalia came down from his darkened office. He told me that he was thinking of collecting his speeches on religion into a book. He asked if I would have a look at them and tell him what I thought. He handed me a large file folder with a copy of the material in it. He kept the originals. I tucked the folder away in my carry-on bag and brought it home to New Orleans.

In lawyerly custom, the first thing I did was to put the speeches into a tabbed white binder. Over the next few months, I read the speeches several times (including once while I was on jury duty). I gave them a light edit, mostly for nits. I did a bit of independent research on various religious subjects. I prepared comments and suggestions for each speech. I made some general observations and suggestions in a transmittal letter. Keeping a copy for myself, I put this white binder, with his speeches and my remarks, into a FedEx box on Thursday, February 11, 2016, for overnight delivery. The binder arrived at the Scalias' home on Friday, February 12, 2016, while Justice Scalia was on his fateful way to a ranch in Texas.

I cannot answer the question why he asked me this favor, or, better, why he bestowed this honor upon me. Justice Scalia had not mentioned the project before, nor had we spent a lot of time talking about religion. I can say now, however, that my acquaintance with these speeches became evidence of what Edmund Burke touchingly called "the unbought grace of life," not to mention, more importantly, a moment of grace in its religious meaning. To me, the speeches are above all else a Catholic's public confession of his faith. To be sure, Justice Scalia's faith was not exactly a secret: he confessed his faith all the time. All the same, that he had made these speeches on religion in the first place, and that he wanted to publish them in a book, bespoke his zeal, his seriousness of purpose to proclaim and bear witness to the faith.

All Christians are called to preach the Gospel to every creature. This does not necessarily entail the use of a soapbox on Speakers' Corner in Hyde Park. Let us examine our consciences, however, stirred as they should be by Justice Scalia's good example: Do I ever acknowledge and speak about my faith to others, including those who do not share it, including also those who are hostile to it? Or do I nearly always avoid such conversations, fearful of adverse social consequences? Is my faith more than a pastime I prefer to golf on Sundays?

Of course, Catholics believe that faith must be proclaimed not merely in words but also in deeds. In one of his speeches, Justice Scalia quotes Matthew 5:48 and wittily reminds us that our good deeds should include even the work that we do:

> "Be thou perfect, as thy heavenly Father is perfect." I think he meant perfect in all things, including that very important thing, the practice of one's life work. . . . Jesus of Nazareth the twenty-nine-year-old carpenter had never put

together a poorly made cabinet. *Laborare est orare*, the old monastic motto goes.

Or, as Reverend Liddell put it in *Chariots of Fire*, "You can praise God by peeling a spud if you peel it to perfection." I don't know about you, but I rarely manage to peel spuds to perfection; and even when I come close, it never occurs to me that my peeling them might be pleasing to God. My dear brother and sister spud peelers: I hope that you will find, as I do, that this basic Christian teaching is helpful, and hopeful, and inspiring, and comforting.

For these moments of grace, and for so much more, I for one owe to Justice Scalia more than I could ever recount, let alone repay.

A. Gregory Grimsal is a lawyer in New Orleans.

Lessons of Faith

BY A. J. BELLIA

Justice Scalia called me mid-morning on a Friday in August 1997. I sat at my desk in a work space upstairs from him at the Supreme Court. I had been on the job as his law clerk for a few weeks but had yet to interact with him in person. Back from travel, he was at the Court. The phone on my desk rang. It was downstairs calling.

"Hello?"

"AJ?" It was him.

"Hello, Justice."

"What's today?"

What's today? Gosh, what is today? It's Friday. He surely knows that. It's August 15. He probably knows that, too. Ah, August 15. Is he asking . . . ? Maybe.

"Justice, it's the Feast of the Assumption."

"Noon?"

"Noon it is."

I assume the justice knew I was Catholic. I was his first clerk from Notre Dame Law School, and my last name rhymed with his. Or maybe he didn't know, and this was his way of inviting me to Mass without inviting me. If I had replied, "Friday," he might have said, "Thanks," and hung up.

No matter. Our walk to noon Mass was one of my first interactions with him. The justice was lively, charming, and funny. When we knelt down in church, however, his face turned solemn. It assumed an expression that, I would later learn, it assumed when things mattered most. In that expression, he removed himself from his surroundings to his thoughts. Anyone who knew him can picture the expression. That day at Mass, the expression held within it a lesson of faith, one of many lessons of faith the justice conveyed by word and example. Here are just a few.

Faith is a gift. Justice Scalia viewed his faith as a gift. The expression he bore at Mass conveyed a sense of gratitude and responsibility. His faith was not a burden. It was not a credit. It was not an artifact. It was a gift, a blessing to be accepted, to be nurtured, to be treasured, to be shared. For those who did not know Justice Scalia and cannot picture this expression, you should imagine the look on the face of someone who has received an unexpected present, one more generous than the occasion required, but one that will require assembly and costly maintenance.

Don't fear being "out of step" (but don't relish it either). The image of a justice in quiet prayer may be "out of step" with general expectations of the noon hour at the Supreme Court. But Justice Scalia never feared being "out of step" with the sensibilities of the day. He said as much, time and again, and he encouraged others to avoid such fear. There's a difference, however, between having the courage to walk out of step and relishing the fact that one is out of step. While Justice Scalia did not fear walking out of step, he never appeared to relish it. He would rather join a majority opinion than write a dissent. He would rather worship in a full church than pray in an empty one. And he would rather keep his heart in friendship with those with whom he disagreed than allow the disagreement to overtake it. Why? Because walking out of step held no value in and of itself. What held value was standing for principle, be it legal principle in a lone dissent or the principle of embracing the goodness that, as a gift of faith, we can see in everyone, disagreement notwithstanding. Don't fear walking out of step. But don't relish it, lest you trample the virtue of friendship. A good lesson for all.

No one is beneath you. Justice Scalia blended into the congregation at Mass as just another pilgrim. No special place. No special seat. It is hard for a Supreme Court Justice to avoid the special place and the special seat. If the nature of the office does not demand special treatment, security likely does. But the justice did not revel in special treatment. One time we tried to take him out for a steak. He wanted a hamburger. Another time we had a seat for him in a luxury box. He wanted a seat in the stands. The justice spoke with the same respect for those in the lowest station as for those in the highest. But it was not a drippy, sentimental, or, worse still, condescending respect. He expected everyone to do the job right, no matter what the job—judging, lawyering, fixing, cleaning. To respect some-one was not to let that someone off the hook. It was to appreciate the potential of all persons, no matter the station, to make good decisions and do a job right. This kind of respect, rooted in the Gospel and the example of Christ, affected him on the job. He did not believe, for example, that questions surrounding the value of life were "known to the nine Justices of this Court any better than they are known to nine people picked at random from the Kansas City telephone directory" (as stated in the concurring opinion in *Cruzan v. Director, Missouri Department of Health*, 1990). As learned as the justice was, he did not believe that elite wisdom, as such, had anything on common wisdom in the pursuit of truth.

Find peace and joy in the truth. The justice found peace and joy in the truth. The Truth. And the truth. For him, the pursuit of truth was not only a matter of faith; it also was a matter of reason. The justice did not view his faith as something divorced from the de-mands of reason. To the contrary, his faith compelled him to embrace the demands of reason in all of life. The justice understood his professional vocation as one of solving legal problems in accord with the rea-sons upon which (he reasoned) judges should act. The justice thoughtfully addressed many questions in his adult life—questions of life, questions of law. As he pondered those questions, his face would assume that familiar expression, a retreat from his surroundings into his thoughts, into a realm where he attempted to solve problems in accord with reason. He'd listen to the voices in the room, process, ponder, listen more, process more, ponder more. Anyone who worked with him will recall the moment when his face softened into a knowing smile. It was the moment he thought he had the answer. That smile was the same smile he wore when he wrote an opinion that wrote itself. He loved the truth, and his smile betrayed the peace and joy he found in its pursuit.

A. J. Bellia, a law professor at Notre Dame Law School, clerked for Justice Scalia during the Supreme Court's October 1997 term.

PART II

POLITICAL LESSONS
FOR BELIEVERS

The Two Kingdoms— Christians and State Authority

Christianity is not a purely private pursuit: the Christian must tend both to his own salvation and to the salvation of others. But government, Justice Scalia argued, is not the Christian means of salvation. The main function of government is the here, not the hereafter.

In a speech in 1989 to an audience of American Catholics in Rome, Justice Scalia explained that the genuine American tradition of separation of church and state is "an authentically Christian tradition as well" and that the confusion of church and state is unhealthy for both institutions. Further, he argued that Christians are morally obligated to obey the laws of just governments.

I want to speak to you this evening about a subject that has been of particular interest to Americans and that Americans have been particularly good at—the relationship between church and state. And I want to look at that subject from each of the particular viewpoints that you and I share: first (and just briefly), from the point of view of citizens of the United States; and second, from the point of view of Roman Catholics.

No principle of American democracy is more fundamental than what has come to be known as the separation of church and state. Unlike many constitutional prescriptions that bear upon individual liberties, this one is reflected not only in the Bill of Rights adopted in 1791—which says that "Congress shall make no law respecting an establishment of religion or prohibiting the free exercise thereof"—but also in the *original* Constitution, which forbids a religious test for federal office.

A separation of church and state was more politically needful in the American republic than elsewhere, because of the sheer diversity of religious views. (A prominent French judge once explained to me the essential difference between France and the United States as follows: France has two religions and three hundred cheeses; the United States has two cheeses and three hundred religions.) But perhaps more than any other principle of American government, that one—the separation of church and state—has swept the Western world. I hope you will excuse my cynicism if I believe that the single most significant cause of that healthy development has been, quite probably, a decline in the vigor of religious belief. Keeping the state out of matters of religion is a much easier political principle for the agnostic than it is for the "true believer" (to use Eric Hoffer's term) of any faith. If one is a skeptic, or not entirely convinced of the truth of one's own religious beliefs, it is quite easy to agree that those beliefs should not be imposed, and indeed should not even be fostered, by the state. After all, they might be wrong. But for the Ayatollah Khomeini—or, for that matter, for devout Christians of the sort who managed the Inquisition—the doctrine is more difficult. If one truly believes that the *hereafter* is all-important, that the pleasures and griefs of our eighty years or so in this world are insignificant except as a means of entering the next, then the temptation is to take whatever action is necessary, including coercive action by the state, to save people—for their own good, whether they know it or not.

In any case, our American political tradition has happily removed this temptation from the path of even the zealous religious believer. It would be wrong to think, however, that the separation of church and state means that the political views of men and women must remain unaffected and uninformed by their religious beliefs. That would be quite impossible to achieve and is assuredly not part of our political tradition. The Declaration of Independence begins by invoking "the Laws of Nature and of Nature's God," and concludes "with a firm reliance on the Protection of Divine Providence." The philosophy expressed in that document, that "all men are endowed *by their Creator* with certain unalienable Rights," underlay the Bill of Rights. Belief in God, leading to that belief in human freedom, had much to do with the greatest war in our national history, as the words of the "Battle Hymn of the Republic" make plain. From abolition to Prohibition, the secular arrangements that Americans have voted for, or indeed fought for, have often been related to their religious beliefs.

It has become fashionable to speak of the American constitutional system as though it contained within itself the philosophy of John Stuart Mill—that everything must be permitted, and nothing can be forbidden, unless it physically harms another human being. That is simply not so. Consider, for example, laws against bigamy, which the Supreme Court has held to be constitutional. Or laws against public nudity. Or laws against cruelty to animals. It cannot be said that any of these prevents physical harm to another human being—or even aesthetic harm of much significance. (If the nudity bothers you, avert your eyes.) It seems to me that society's desire for laws of this sort—and all societies have them—is traceable to some common ethos, either religiously based or indistinguishable from religious prescription, which the old writers used to call *bonos mores*—"good morals." The most difficult task of constitutional adjudication in modern times, when these shared values are less uniform than they once were, is to decide how far the state can go in preserving a common fabric of morality.

Though its commands may be vague at the margins, however, our American tradition of separation of church and state is in its essentials firm and clear. I intend to address most of my remarks this evening to the subject of church and state looked at from the other perspective that you and I share, the perspective of a Roman Catholic. There the outlines are not as clear—but I think they ought to be. It seems to me (and I think I am not impressing my American notions upon the matter) that our faith's message on the subject is essentially the same as that of the Constitution: church and state are separate. One can reason at least partway to the conclusion, I suppose, theologically: state coercion of religious belief is wrong because it suppresses the free will that is precisely the respect in which man is made, as we say, "in the image of God." It is not possible to save someone "in spite of himself." But I think the revealed word of God in the Gospels goes much further than this modest point and displays a vision of the separate sphere of operation of church and state that is similar to what the Founding Fathers produced.

The strongest evidence—and Christ's only explicit statement on the subject—is the well-known exchange with the Pharisees on the subject of taxes. Knowing the Jews' hatred of Roman rule, and the religious scruples of many of them against paying taxes to a heathen emperor who styled himself a god, the Pharisees asked Christ whether it was lawful—that is, lawful under the Jewish religious law—to pay tribute to Caesar. A question, it seemed, which had no answer that would not be damaging to Jesus's cause in one way or another: either by alienating devout Jews, or by making himself an enemy of the Roman state. As you recall, he asked the Pharisees to show him a coin and inquired whose image was on it. When the answer came back "Caesar's," he delivered that devastating line, "Render unto God the things that are God's and unto Caesar the things that are Caesar's." It was, in modern terms, a stopper. As St. Luke records it, "marvelling at his answer, they kept silence."

But it was, of course, more than just a snappy comeback. Christ said it not only because it was a hard point to answer, but because it was true. The business of the state, he was saying, is not God's business. Not that the state is in any way inherently evil; or that there are not good governments and bad governments insofar as pursuing the proper ends of government is concerned; or that some governments are not more conducive to their citizens' service of God than others. But in the last analysis the most important objectives of human existence—goodness, virtue, godliness, salvation—are not achieved through the state; and those who seek them there are doomed to disappointment.

The Gospels are so full of that message that it is surprising it can be so readily ignored. St. John records, for example, that after Jesus fed the five thousand with five barley loaves and two fishes, the crowd was so impressed that they wanted to make him king. Not a bad post, one would think, if the state were particularly useful for achieving the most important things Christ was after. John records Christ's reaction to that prospect as follows: "When Jesus perceived that they would come to take him by force and make him king, he fled again to the mountain, himself alone."

Or, of course, the memorable interview with the

Roman procurator Pilate—almost a personification of confrontation between religion and government, displaying so succinctly how little the latter understands the former. Pilate asks Jesus whether it's true that he's a king. Jesus replies—I have always thought it a very playful reply under the circumstances—Did you come to this conclusion on your own, or did somebody tell you? And Pilate bristles. "Am I a Jew?" Jesus then goes on to talk about his kingdom. "My kingdom is not of this world. If my kingdom were of this world, my followers would have fought that I might not be delivered. . . . But, as it is, my kingdom is not from here." Pilate replies, in effect, "So you admit you're a king," and Jesus answers: "Thou sayest it; I am a king. This is why I was born, and why I have come into the world, to bear witness to the truth." And Pilate ends the interview with that sad line—so expressive of the cynicism that comes with power, then as now—"What is truth?"

It could not be clearer from all of this that the state is not the Christian's source of power, nor his means of salvation. The fundamental reason, I suggest, is also clear from the Gospels: that the focus of concern of the two kingdoms is fundamentally different. A good government should not, to be sure, impede the religious practices of its people; it ought indeed, as many of the decisions of our Supreme Court have said, accommodate those practices where possible. But its main function is not the hereafter but the here: assuring a safe, just, and prosperous society. Contrast that with

the main function of the kingdom Christ was referring to. I mentioned a little earlier the feeding of the
five thousand. The Gospels mention a similar incident
in which Christ fed four thousand. How significant,
I have always thought, that they mention no others.
From all indications, there was plenty of poverty in
Judea in those days—yet Christ chooses to alleviate
it by miraculous means only twice, in circumstances
in which the object of the exercise is to show his compassion and his power rather than to end once and for
all the hardship of a poor country. How different from
the way Caesar would—and should—have acted if he
possessed the same power. The central concerns of
their kingdoms were, you see, quite different. Caesar
would never have said—*should* never have said—the
following:

> [D]o not be anxious for your life, what you shall
> eat; nor yet for your body, what you shall put on.
> The life is a greater thing than the food, and the
> body than the clothing. . . .
>
> Consider how the lilies grow; they neither toil
> nor spin, yet I say to you that not even Solomon
> in all his glory was arrayed like one of these.
> But if God so clothes the grass which flourishes
> in the field today but tomorrow is thrown into
> the oven, how much more you, O you of little
> faith! . . .
>
> [D]o not seek what you shall eat, or what you

shall drink. . . . But seek the kingdom of God,
and all these things shall be given you besides.

I suggest that, coming from a temporal ruler, that
would be a perfect recipe for national disaster. It is assuredly the business of the state to be concerned about
precisely those things.

I hope you will not mistake what I am saying. My
point is not that the Christian has no concern for how
government operates, or what it achieves. Of course
he does. In everything he performs, from baseball to
government, the Christian is supposed to put on the
mind of Christ, which includes a concern for all his fellow men. So a government that serves the interests of
the few at the expense of the many is to that extent an
un-Christian government. But to fix upon good government as the objective, or even the principal mani-
festation, of Christianity is to give the business I am
in more credit than it deserves—and to miss the point
of the faith. Rulers who do not follow Christian principles—of justice, of unselfishness, and of charity—
have *personally* much to account for; but they do not
necessarily rule over a less Christian society. And vice
versa: rulers who follow Christian principles may well
store up merit for *themselves* in the next world; but
they do not necessarily bring the Kingdom of God to
their subjects.

I may digress momentarily to make the related observation that Christian principles in the context of

government do not coincide with Christian principles in the context of personal morality. For when government acts, it does not act merely as one of God's creatures dealing with another of God's creatures of equal worth and dignity; rather, if it is a lawful government, it acts (as I shall discuss at greater length later) pursuant to God's authority and indeed on His behalf. What is Christian morality in person-to-person dealings, therefore, is not necessarily Christian morality in dealings between the government and those lawfully subject to its power. Christ says, of person-to-person dealings, that if a person should steal your cloak, give him your tunic as well. Could a state possibly operate on such a principle? He says, of person-to-person dealings, that we should forgive him who wrongs us seven times seventy times. Could a criminal-law system possibly heed this advice? The epitome of personal Christian perfection is to distribute all one's worldly goods to the poor; but that does not translate to the proposition that the epitome of Christian government is communism (with or without official atheism)—any more than the personal Christian virtue of poverty translates to a governmental Christian virtue of poverty.

But to return to my principal thesis: preoccupation with government misses the point—which is not the material salvation of the society, but the spiritual welfare of individual souls. To acquire a theological fixation upon the former is ultimately to distort the Gospel message. That is, by the way, the sort of distortion that has probably always occurred. We tend to remember how ideas about religion have influenced government, but to forget how ideas about government have influenced religion. A single example will suffice: In the nineteenth century, when individualistic capitalism was the governmental ideal, the churches stressed the Christian virtues of honesty, hard work, and self-denial. Charity, compassion, and love of the poor were acknowledged to be Christian virtues as well—but they were not emphasized. In the twentieth century, the century in which socialism rather than capitalism dominated governmental theory, the priorities were reversed: charity, compassion, and love of the poor were stressed; and the more Calvinistic values of honesty, hard work, and self-denial were seldom heard. Those theologians who think we have corrected the errors of the past are mistaken. We are just repeating, in this century as in the last, the error of accommodating the Gospel to the secular ideology of the time.

In sum, our American tradition that church and state are separate is in my view an authentically Christian tradition as well. There are good religious reasons for it as well as good political reasons; the confusion of the two hurts *both*. Sectarian struggles for control can destroy the state; and religious preoccupation with government—with material welfare, with power, with coercion—can destroy the church.

The second point I want to make, in looking at the church-state relationship from the standpoint of our religion, is that the Christian bears a moral obligation toward the just state. It is popular in some revisionist histories to portray Jesus as (literally) a Zealot—one of a band of Jewish rebels against Roman rule. Of course his remark about rendering to Caesar contradicts that—as does his remark to the Roman procurator after the scourging: "You could have no power at all over me, unless it had been given you from above." Far from being a revolutionary, Christ seems to have been more deferential to lawful authority than most Christian Americans I know these days. Nor were the apostles contemptuous of government, even pagan Roman government. Consider Paul's letter to the Romans:

> Let everyone be subject to the higher authorities, for there exists no authority except from God, and those who exist have been appointed by God. Therefore he who resists the authority resists the ordinance of God; and they that resist bring on themselves condemnation. For rulers are a terror not to the good work but to the evil. Dost thou wish, then, not to fear the authority? Do what is good and thou wilt have praise from it. For it is God's minister to thee for good. But if thou dost what is evil, fear, for not without reason does it carry the sword. For it is God's minister, an avenger to execute wrath on him who does evil. Wherefore you must needs be subject, not only because of the wrath, but also for conscience' sake. For this is also why you

pay tribute, for they are the ministers of God, serving unto this very end. Render to all men whatever is their due; tribute to whom tribute is due; taxes to whom taxes are due; fear to whom fear is due; honor to whom honor is due.

The passage must be read to refer to lawful authority, of course—and there is plenty of room to argue that some authorities that are *de facto* in place are not lawful ones, either because of how they got there, or because of what they did when they arrived. It is not those details to which I wish to direct your attention, however, but rather to the central proposition that, for the Christian, lawful civil authority must be obeyed not merely out of fear but, as St. Paul says, for conscience' sake.

That proposition was once widely accepted. I recall reading, a few years ago, an essay of C. S. Lewis that simply assumed, without significant discussion, that a good Christian who had been guilty of a serious criminal offense would turn himself in. Lewis used the now-quaint expression "pay his just debt to society." That attitude is long gone—mostly, I think, because we have lost the perception, expressed in that passage from St. Paul, that the laws have a moral claim to our obedience.

That truth is greatly obscured in an age of democratic government. It was once easy, perhaps, to regard God as the ultimate source of the authority of a hereditary king, whose bloodline reached back to the mists of history—where, for all one knew, God did anoint his forebear. It is even easy to see the hand of God in the accession of a new ruler through the fury of battle, whose awesomeness and unpredictability seem to display the working of the Lord of Hosts. It is more difficult to regard God as making His will known through PACs, thirty-second spots, Gallup polls, and voting machines. And even apart from the less-than-Jehovian process of election, the fundamental principle of *vox populi, vox dei* has never been a very persuasive proposition. How hard it is to accept the notion that those knaves and fools whom we voted against, but who succeeded in hoodwinking a majority of the electorate, will enact and promulgate laws and directives that, unless they contravene moral precepts, divine law enjoins us to obey.

It is particularly hard for someone in the American democratic tradition to have the proper Christian attitude toward lawful civil authority. We are a nation largely settled by those fleeing from oppressive regimes, and there is in our political tradition a deep strain of the notion that government is, at best, a necessary evil. But no society, least of all a democracy, can long survive on that philosophy. It is fine to believe that good government is limited government, but it is disabling—and, I suggest, contrary to long and sound Christian teaching—to believe that all government is bad. It is true, of course, that those who hold high office are, in their human nature and dignity, no better than the least of those whom they govern; that government by men and women is, of necessity, an imperfect enterprise; that power tends to corrupt; that a free society must be ever vigilant against abuse of governmental authority; and that institutional checks and balances against unbridled power are essential to preserve democracy. But it is also true that just government has a *moral* claim—that is, a divinely prescribed claim—to our obedience. It is not an easy truth, because as Eden showed, obedience is not an easy virtue.

Politics and the Public Good—the False Allure of Socialism

In this 1996 speech at the Pontifical Gregorian University in Rome, Justice Scalia addressed the question "Is the political philosophy of the Left or of the Right more compatible with the public good?" He observed that socialism holds an allure for some Christians because it seems to mean well, but, he explained, that allure is deceptive.

If there was ever a topic that cried out for a definition of terms, it is this one. "Right" and "left," "right-wing" and "left-wing" are terms that have virtually no fixed meaning in American political discourse, except that they all connote (as they do not in European political discourse) a degree of extremism. In America, both categories of term are pejorative. Thus, we have in American political commentary that familiar villain, the "right-wing extremist"; and, more recently, that ominous political force, the "Christian right." The terms "left-wing extremist" and "Christian left" would have similar overtones of foreboding if they were ever used by the American media—but they are not, which is an interesting phenomenon.

Once one gets beyond their pejorative content, it is hard to pin down the meaning of "right" and "left" in American political usage. Sometimes they are used to denote, respectively, statists and libertarians—those who favor strong and authoritarian government versus those who favor a high degree of individual freedom. In this sense, Richard Nixon would be a man of the Right and Eugene McCarthy a man of the Left. But if those were the only meanings of the terms, both Augusto Pinochet and Fidel Castro would have to be referred to as right-wingers. A second, quite different, connotation of the terms uses them to distinguish between laissez-faire capitalists and socialists. This is not only different from, but sometimes the opposite of, the first connotation—since those who favor a high degree of individual freedom in other matters often favor a high degree of individual freedom in economic matters as well. Thus, the American Libertarian Party is a party of the Left under the first connotation, and a party of the Right under the second.

Yet a third meaning of "right" and "left" is much more relativistic: it draws a distinction between those who favor the *status quo* and those who favor change—between conservatives and progressives. Since over most of the past century change has been moving from a *status quo* of capitalism toward socialism, this third connotation tends to produce the same results as the second—Castro can be called a man of the Left in both these senses. But if and when the tide of history moves in reverse, the equivalence between the two connotations disappears. The old-line Communists in Russia, who resist the change toward democracy and capitalism, are referred to in the American press (believe it or not) as the "Right." And finally, "right" and "left" may connote a distinction between nationalism and one-worldism. This may be merely one aspect of the first connotation I mentioned: those who favor a strong, authoritarian government are ordinarily nationalists. But it really must be an entirely separate connotation, since I can think of no other basis for calling Nazis a party of the Right and Communists a party of the Left. They are both authoritarian, they are both socialist, and they are both untraditional; but the Communists are internationalists.

For purposes of my remarks today, I am assuming the second meaning of "right" and "left," the meaning that refers to the difference between capitalism and socialism. I take that approach in part because that probably comes closest to the meaning of the terms in European political discourse, and thus is more likely to be what the conveners of this conference had in mind; and in part because that is the only one of the dichotomies I have mentioned that is the subject of widespread current debate. In the waning years of the twentieth century, few have been urging a return to authoritarianism, vigorous nationalism, or traditionalism, whereas capitalism has made something of a comeback.

I must make a second clarification about the subject of my remarks. I have chosen to interpret "the common good" to mean "the Christian common good." Thus, I take that system to be conducive to the common good which is conducive to virtue (as Christianity understands virtue) and sanctification. I assume that this is the meaning of "the common good" that the organizers of the conference had in mind—the Gregorianum being, as I understand it, a school of theology and not of government or economics.

Having fully defined my topic, the first thing I wish to say about it is that I do not believe in it. That is to say, I do not believe that a Christian ought to choose his form of government on the basis of which will be most conducive to his faith, any more than he ought to choose a toothpaste on that basis. To be sure, there are certain prohibitions. A Christian should not support a government that suppresses the faith, or one that sanctions the taking of innocent human life— just as a Christian should not wear immodest clothes. But the test of good government, like the test of good tailoring, is assuredly *not* whether it helps you save your soul. Government is not meant for saving souls, but for protecting life and property and ensuring the conditions for physical prosperity. Its responsibility is the here, not the hereafter—and the needs of the two sometimes diverge. It may well be, for example, that a governmental system which keeps its citizens in relative poverty will produce more saints. (The rich, as Christ said, have a harder time getting to heaven.) But that would be a bad government, nonetheless. This recognition of the separate spheres of church and state is not just the teaching of the First Amendment to the United States Constitution. It is also, I think, the teaching of Jesus Christ—who spoke of rendering to Caesar the things that are Caesar's and is not recorded as having indicated any preference about government, except one: He did not want the people to make *Him* king.

If I were to engage in the search for the form of government most conducive to Christianity, however, I would certainly not settle upon the candidate that seems to have such a great attraction for modern Catholic thinkers: socialism. It is hard to understand that attraction. Surely it does not rest upon the teachings of experience. I know of no country in which the churches have grown fuller as the governments have moved leftward. The churches of Europe are empty. The most religious country in the West by all standards—belief in God, church membership, church attendance—is that bastion of capitalism least diluted by socialism, the United States.

When I say least diluted by socialism, you must understand that I say it in a modern context, in which we are all socialists. In the United States, that battle was fought and decided with the New Deal. No one, even in the most conservative quarters of American society, now denies that there should be a so-called safety net provided by the government for our citizens. The only real argument is over how many services that safety net should provide, and how poor one must be in order to qualify. Few of us even understand anymore what a truly non-socialist mentality was like. I happened to encounter it, by accident, when I was a young law professor, doing research for an article on sovereign immunity—the legal doctrine that says that a state cannot be sued without its consent. I came across a debate in the Massachusetts legislature, during the eighteenth century, concerning a proposed bill that would provide compensation to a woman who had been seriously injured through the negligence of one of the agents of the state—a policeman, or a fireman, or whatever. Those members of the Massachusetts legislature opposing the legislation argued that they *had no right*—that it was *morally wrong*—to use public funds for private benefit, for a purpose that did not benefit the public at large. Because of the doctrine of sovereign immunity, they argued, the Commonwealth of Massachusetts owed this woman nothing in law, and to agree to pay her, out of public funds, money that was not legally owed was in effect to use public funds for a private gift, which (they said) was wrong. And this, I point out, was a woman *who had been injured* by the commonwealth; you can imagine what their attitude would have been toward dispensing public funds to the poor!

In the United States, a remnant of that non-socialist attitude lasted into the present century. Our federal Constitution, you may recall, gives Congress not a general power to expend funds, but only the power to expend funds "for the general welfare." Until the triumph of the New Deal, there were many who thought that prohibited the expenditure of funds for any private assistance. Neither to the rich, nor to the poor. But that fight, as I have said, is over. We now believe that any expenditure for any citizen is an expenditure for the general welfare—whether to the poor, such as food-stamp recipients; or to the middle class or even fairly well-to-do, such as the victims of a tornado in Florida; or even to the downright rich, such as shareholders of Chrysler Corporation. All of these are now regarded as entirely proper objects of the state's beneficence.

The allure of socialism for the Christian, I think, is that it means well; it is, or appears to be, altruistic. It promises assistance from the state for the poor, and public provision of all the necessities of life, from maternity care to geriatric care, and from kindergarten through university. Capitalism, on the other hand, promises nothing from the state except the opportunity to succeed or fail. Adam Smith points unabashedly to the fact that the baker does not provide bread out of the goodness of his heart, but for profit. How uninspiring. Yet if you reflect upon it, you will see that the socialistic message is not necessarily Christian, and the capitalist message not necessarily non-Christian. The issue is not whether there should be provision for the poor, but rather the degree to which that provision should be made through the coercive power of the state. Christ said, after all, that you should give *your* goods to the poor, not that you should force someone else to give *his*.

Bear in mind that in this discussion I am not arguing about whether socialism is good or bad *as a system of government*. If private charity does not suffice to meet the needs of the poor, or if we do not want the poor to have to regard themselves as the objects of charity, or if we even wish to go beyond merely assisting the poor and want to redistribute the wealth of the rich to the middle class, socialism may be a better way to meet worldly needs. But that can be decided on the economic and secular merits of the matter. The question I am asking is whether Christian faith must incline us toward that system, and the answer, I think, is no. Christ did not preach "a chicken in every pot," or "the elimination of poverty in our lifetime"; those are worldly, governmental goals. If they were His objectives, He certainly devoted little of His time and talent to achieving them—feeding the hungry multitudes only a couple of times, as I recall, and running away from the crowds who wanted to put Him on the throne, where He would have had an opportunity to engage in some real redistribution of wealth. His message was not the need to eliminate hunger, or misery, or misfortune, but rather the need for each individual to love and help the hungry, the miserable, and the unfortunate. To the extent the state takes upon itself one of the corporal works of mercy that could and would have been undertaken privately, it deprives individuals of an opportunity for sanctification and deprives the body of Christ of an occasion for the interchange of love among its members.

I wonder to what extent the decimation of women's religious orders throughout the West is attributable to the governmentalization of charity. Consider how many orphanages, hospitals, schools, and homes for the elderly were provided by orders of nuns. They are almost all gone; the state provides or pays for these services. Even purely individual charity must surely have been affected. What need for me to give a beggar a handout? Do I not pay taxes for government food stamps and municipally run shelters and soup kitchens? The man asking me for a dollar probably wants it for liquor. There is, of course, neither any love nor any merit in the taxes I pay for those services; I pay them under compulsion.

The governmentalization of charity affects not just the donor but also the recipient. What was once asked as a favor is now demanded as an entitlement. When I was young, there used to be an expression applied to a lazy person: "He thinks the world owes him a living." But the teaching of welfare socialism is that the world does owe everyone a living. This belief must affect the character of welfare recipients—and not, I suggest, for the better. Or at least not for the better in the distinctively Christian view of things. Christ's special love for the poor was attributable to one quality that they possessed in abundance: meekness and humility. It is humbling to be an object of charity—which is why mendicant nuns and friars used to beg. The transformation of charity into legal entitlement has produced both donors without love and recipients without gratitude.

It has also produced a change in the product that is distributed. Most particularly, and most relevantly for purposes of the present discussion, social services distributed by the state in my country, for example, cannot be intermingled with Christian teaching, or even (increasingly) with Christian morality. They do not say the Angelus in public orphanages; there are no crucifixes on the walls of public hospitals; and the Ten Commandments are not posted in public schools. The religiously driven and religiously funded social welfare movements of the nineteenth century sought to achieve not merely the alleviation of poverty and hardship, but also what was called moral uplift. Of course that is no part of the function of state-administered social welfare today. The state-paid social worker, whose job is to see to the distribution of welfare funds to those who are legally entitled to them, is not— cannot legally be—concerned with improving not only the diet but also the virtue of her "clients" (which is the coldly commercial terminology that welfare bureaucracies use). It is quite simply none of her business.

Perhaps the clearest effects of the expansion of the state accompanied by the contraction of the church are to be found in the field of primary and secondary education. A relatively small proportion of Americans are nowadays educated in religious schools; Catholic schools are much less numerous than they were in mid-century. As the costs of primary and secondary education have risen, it has become very difficult for churches to run a system competitive with the tax-funded public schools. Simultaneously, litigation has caused the public schools to eliminate all religiously doctrinal materials from their curriculum. That is good and proper under our American system, which forbids the official establishment of any sect. But the non-sectarian state's increasing monopoly over primary and secondary education can hardly be considered beneficial to Christianity. Whereas such overtly religious texts as *The Pilgrim's Progress* were once the staple of the American schoolchild's education, religious instruction, if received at all, is obtained one evening a week in confraternity classes, or on Sunday. In more recent years, as society has become more and more diverse in its views on morality, the state's control of education deprives children not only of Catholic doctrine, but even of essentially Catholic moral formation. Schools distribute condoms, provide advice on birth control and abortion, and teach that homosexuality must not be regarded as shameful or abnormal. Again, it is not my place or my purpose to criticize these developments, only to observe that they do not suggest that expanding the role of government is good for Christianity.

Finally, I may mention that even the seeming Christian virtue of socialism—that it *means* well and seeks to help the poor—may be greatly exaggerated. It is true in the United States, and I believe it is true in all of the Western democracies, that the vast bulk of social spending does not go to the poor, but rather to the middle class (which also happens to be the class most numerous at the polls). The most expensive entitlement programs, Social Security and Medicare, for example, overwhelmingly benefit those who are not in dire financial straits. So one may plausibly argue that welfare-state democracy does not really have even the Christian virtue of altruism. The majority does not say to the rich, "Give your money to the poor," but rather, "Give your money to us."

Just as I believe the Left is not necessarily endowed with Christian virtue, so also I believe the Right is not necessarily bereft of it. Laissez-faire capitalism, like socialism, speaks to the degree of involvement of the state in the economic life of the society. Like socialism also, it does not speak to the nature of the human soul. There have been greedy and avaricious capitalists, but there have also been generous and considerate ones; just as there have been altruistic and self-deprecating socialists, but have also been brutal and despotic ones. The cardinal sin of capitalism is greed; but the cardinal sin of socialism is power. I am not sure there is a clear choice between those evils.

While I would not argue that capitalism as an economic system is inherently more Christian than socialism (so long as we are talking about a form of socialism that permits the acquisition and ownership of property), it does seem to me that capitalism is more *dependent* upon Christianity than socialism is. For in order for capitalism to work—in order for it to produce a good and a stable society—the Christian virtues are essential. Since in the capitalist system each individual has more freedom of action, each individual also has more opportunity to do evil. Without widespread practice of such Christian virtues as honesty, self-denial, and charity toward others, a capitalist system will be intolerable.

Let me conclude as I began, with a disclaimer: the burden of my remarks is not that a government of the Right is more Christ-like, only that there is no reason to believe that a government of the Left is. To tell you the truth, I do not think Christ cares very much what sort of economic or political system we live under. He certainly displayed little interest in that subject during His time among us—as did His apostles. Accordingly, we should select our economic and political systems on the basis of what seems to produce the greatest material good for the greatest number, and leave theology out of it. The minimum wage, for example—which is a current political issue in Washington—is a good or a bad idea depending upon whether it produces good or bad economic consequences. It has nothing to do with the Kingdom of God.

The Authority of Government—Catholics and the Death Penalty

The modern view that the death penalty is immoral, Justice Scalia argued, has little to do with the West's Christian tradition and everything to do with the fact that the West is the home of democracy. It is difficult to see the hand of God behind those we elect, so it is tempting—but mistaken—to doubt the moral authority of a democratic government.

In these extensive excerpts from a speech—published as an article ("God's Justice and Ours") in First Things *in 2002—Justice Scalia examined recent Catholic opposition to the death penalty in the context of "two thousand years of Christian teaching."*

Before proceeding to discuss the morality of capital punishment, I want to make clear that my views on the subject have nothing to do with how I vote in capital cases that come before the Supreme Court. That statement would not be true if I subscribed to the conventional fallacy that the Constitution is a "living document"—that is, a text that means from age to age whatever the society (or perhaps the Court) thinks it ought to mean.

But while my views on the morality of the death penalty have nothing to do with how I vote as a judge, they have a lot to do with whether I can or should be a judge at all. To put the point in the blunt terms employed by Justice Harry Blackmun toward the end of his career on the bench, when he announced that he would henceforth vote (as Justices William Brennan and Thurgood Marshall had previously done) to overturn all death sentences, when I sit on a Court that reviews and affirms capital convictions, I am part of "the machinery of death." My vote, when joined with at least four others, is, in most cases, the last step that permits an execution to proceed. I could not take part in that process if I believed what was being done to be immoral.

Capital cases are much different from the other life-and-death issues that my Court sometimes faces: abortion, for example, or legalized suicide. There it is not the state (of which I am in a sense the last instrument) that is decreeing death, but rather private individuals whom the state has decided not to restrain. One may argue (as many do) that the society has a moral obligation to restrain. That moral obligation may weigh heavily upon the voter, and upon the legislator who enacts the laws; but a judge, I think, bears no moral guilt for the laws society has failed to enact. Thus, my difficulty with *Roe v. Wade* is a legal rather than a moral one: I do not believe (and, for two hundred years, no one believed) that the Constitution contains a right to abortion. And if a state were to permit abortion on demand, I would—and could in good conscience—vote against an attempt to invalidate that law for the same reason that I vote against the invalidation of laws that forbid abortion on demand: because the Constitution gives the federal government (and hence me) no power over the matter.

With the death penalty, on the other hand, I am part of the criminal-law machinery that imposes death— which extends from the indictment, to the jury conviction, to rejection of the last appeal. I am aware of the ethical principle that one can give "material cooperation" to the immoral act of another when the evil that would attend failure to cooperate is even greater (for example, helping a burglar tie up a householder where the alternative is that the burglar would kill the householder). I doubt whether that doctrine is even applicable to the trial judges and jurors who must themselves determine that the death sentence will be imposed. It seems to me these individuals are not merely engaged in "material cooperation" with someone else's action, but are themselves decreeing death on behalf of the state.

It is a matter of great consequence to me, therefore, whether the death penalty is morally acceptable. As a Roman Catholic—and being unable to jump out of my skin—I cannot discuss that issue without reference to Christian tradition and the Church's Magisterium.

The death penalty is undoubtedly wrong unless one accords to the state a scope of moral action that goes beyond what is permitted to the individual. In my view, the major impetus behind modern aversion to the death penalty is the equation of private morality with governmental morality. This is a predictable (though I believe erroneous and regrettable) reaction to modern, democratic self-government.

Few doubted the morality of the death penalty in the age that believed in the divine right of kings. Or even in earlier times. St. Paul had this to say (I am quoting, as you might expect, the King James Version):

> Let every soul be subject unto the higher powers. For there is no power but of God: the powers that be are ordained of God. Whosoever therefore resisteth the power, resisteth the ordinance of God: and they that resist shall receive to themselves damnation. For rulers are not a terror to good works, but to the evil. Wilt thou then not be afraid of the power? Do that which is good, and thou shalt have praise of the same: for he is the minister of God to thee for good. But if thou do that which is evil, be afraid; for he beareth not the sword in vain: for he is the minister of God, a revenger to execute wrath upon him that doeth evil. Wherefore ye must needs be subject, not only for wrath, but also for conscience' sake. (Romans 13:1–5)

This is not the Old Testament, I emphasize, but St. Paul. One can understand his words as referring only to lawfully constituted authority, or even only to lawfully constituted authority that rules justly. But the *core* of his message is that government—however you want to limit that concept—derives its moral authority from God. It is the "minister of God" with powers to "revenge," to "execute wrath," including even wrath by the sword (which is unmistakably a reference to the death penalty). Paul of course did not believe that the *individual* possessed any such powers. Only a few lines before this passage, he wrote, "Dearly beloved, avenge not yourselves, but rather give place unto wrath: for it is written, Vengeance is mine; I will repay, saith the Lord." And in this world the Lord repaid—did justice— through His minister, the state.

These passages from Romans represent the consensus of Western thought until very recent times. Not just of Christian or religious thought, but of secular thought regarding the powers of the state. That consensus has been upset, I think, by the emergence of democracy. It is easy to see the hand of the Almighty behind rulers whose forebears, in the dim mists of history, were supposedly anointed by God, or who at least obtained their thrones in awful and unpredictable battles whose outcome was determined by the Lord of Hosts, that is, the Lord of Armies. It is much more difficult to see the hand of God—or any higher moral authority—behind the fools and rogues (as the losers would have it) whom we ourselves elect to do our own will. How can their power to avenge—to vindicate the "public order"—be any greater than our own?

So it is no accident, I think, that the modern view

that the death penalty is immoral is centered in the West. That has little to do with the fact that the West has a Christian tradition, and everything to do with the fact that the West is the home of democracy. Indeed, it seems to me that the more Christian a country is, the *less* likely it is to regard the death penalty as immoral. Abolition has taken its firmest hold in post-Christian Europe and has least support in the churchgoing United States. I attribute that to the fact that, for the believing Christian, death is no big deal. Intentionally killing an innocent person is a big deal: it is a grave sin, which causes one to lose his soul. But losing this life, in exchange for the next? The Christian attitude is reflected in the words Robert Bolt's play has Thomas More saying to the headsman: "Friend, be not afraid of your office. You send me to God." And when Cranmer asks whether he is sure of that, More replies, "He will not refuse one who is so blithe to go to Him." For the non-believer, on the other hand, to deprive a man of his life is to end his existence. What a horrible act!

Besides being *less* likely to regard death as an utterly cataclysmic punishment, the Christian is also *more* likely to regard punishment in general as deserved. The doctrine of free will—the ability of man to resist temptations to evil, which God will not permit beyond man's capacity to resist—is central to the Christian doctrine of salvation and damnation, heaven and hell. The post-Freudian secularist, on the other hand, is more inclined to think that people are what their history and circumstances have made them, and there is little sense in assigning blame.

Of course those who deny the authority of a government to exact vengeance are not entirely logical. Many crimes—for example, domestic murder in the heat of passion—are neither deterred by punishment meted out to others nor likely to be committed a second time by the same offender. Yet opponents of capital punishment do not object to sending such an offender to prison, perhaps for life. Because he *deserves* punishment. Because it is *just*.

The mistaken tendency to believe that a democratic government, being nothing more than the composite will of its individual citizens, has no more moral power or authority than they do as individuals has adverse effects in other areas as well. It fosters civil disobedience, for example, which proceeds on the assumption that what the individual citizen considers an unjust law—even if it does not compel *him* to act unjustly—need not be obeyed. St. Paul would not agree. "Ye must needs be subject," he said, "not only for wrath, but also for conscience' sake." For conscience' sake. The reaction of people of faith to this tendency of democracy to obscure the divine authority behind government should not be resignation to it, but the resolution to combat it as effectively as possible. We have done that in this country (and continental Europe has not) by preserving in our public life many visible reminders that—in the words of a Supreme Court opinion from the 1940s—"we are a religious people, whose institutions presuppose a Supreme Being." These reminders include: "In God we trust" on our coins, "one nation, under God" in our Pledge of Allegiance, the opening of sessions of our legislatures with a prayer, the opening of sessions of my Court with "God save the United States and this Honorable Court," annual Thanksgiving proclamations issued by our president at the direction of Congress, and constant invocations of divine support in the speeches of our political leaders, which often conclude, "God bless America." All this, as I say, is most un-European, and helps explain why our people are more inclined to understand, as St. Paul did, that government carries the sword as "the minister of God," to "execute wrath" upon the evildoer.

It will come as no surprise from what I have said that I do not agree with the encyclical *Evangelium vitae* and the new Catholic catechism (or the very latest version of the new Catholic catechism), according to which the death penalty can be imposed only to protect rather than avenge, and that since it is (in most modern societies) not necessary for the former purpose, it is wrong. That, by the way, is how I read those documents—and not, as Avery Cardinal Dulles would read them, simply as an affirmation of two millennia of Christian teaching that retribution is a proper purpose (indeed, the principal purpose) of criminal punishment, but merely adding the "prudential judgment" that in modern circumstances condign retribution "rarely if ever" justifies death. I cannot square that interpretation with the following passage from the encyclical:

> It is clear that, for these [permissible purposes of penal justice] to be achieved, the nature and extent of the punishment must be carefully evaluated and decided upon, and ought not go to the extreme of executing the offender except in cases of absolute necessity: *in other words, when it would not be possible otherwise to defend society. Today, however, as a result of steady improvements in the organization of the penal system, such cases are very rare, if not practically nonexistent.* (Emphases deleted and added.)

It is true enough that the paragraph of the encyclical that precedes this passage acknowledges (in accord with traditional Catholic teaching) that "the primary purpose of the punishment which society inflicts is 'to redress the disorder caused by the offense'" by "imposing on the offender an adequate punishment for the crime." But it seems to me quite impossible to interpret the later passage's phrase "when it would not be possible otherwise to defend society" as including "defense" through the redress of disorder achieved by adequate punishment. Not only does the word "defense" not readily lend itself to that strange interpretation, but the immediately following explanation of why, in modern times, "defense" rarely if ever requires capital punishment *has no bearing whatever upon the adequacy of retribution.* In fact, one might say that it has an *inverse* bearing.

How in the world can modernity's "steady improvements in the organization of the penal system" render the death penalty less condign for a particularly heinous crime? One might think that commitment to a really horrible penal system (Devil's Island, for example) might be almost as bad as death. But nice clean cells with television sets, exercise rooms, meals designed by nutritionists, and conjugal visits? That would seem to render the death penalty more, rather than less, necessary. So also would the greatly increased capacity for evil—the greatly increased power to produce moral "disorder"—placed in individual hands by modern technology. Could St. Paul or St. Thomas even have envisioned a crime by an individual (as opposed to one by a ruler, such as Herod's slaughter of the innocents) as enormous as that of Timothy McVeigh or of the men who destroyed three thousand innocents in the World Trade Center? If just retribution is a legitimate purpose (indeed, the principal legitimate purpose) of capital punishment, can one possibly say with a straight face that nowadays death would "rarely if ever" be appropriate?

So I take the encyclical and the latest, hot-off-the-presses version of the catechism (a supposed encapsulation of the "deposit" of faith and the Church's teaching regarding a moral order that does not change) to mean that retribution is not a valid purpose of capital punishment. Unlike such other hard Catholic doctrines as the prohibition of birth control and of abortion, this is not a moral position that the Church has always—or indeed *ever before*—maintained. There have been Christian opponents of the death penalty, just as there have been Christian pacifists, but neither of those positions has ever been that of the Church. The current predominance of opposition to the death penalty is the legacy of Napoleon, Hegel, and Freud rather than St. Paul and St. Augustine. I mentioned earlier Thomas More, who has long been regarded in this country as the patron saint of lawyers, and who has recently been declared by the Vatican the patron saint of politicians (I am not sure that is a promotion). One of the charges leveled by that canonized saint's detractors was that, as lord chancellor, he was too quick to impose the death penalty.

I am therefore happy to learn from the canonical experts I have consulted that the position set forth in *Evangelium vitae* and in the latest version of the Catholic catechism does not purport to be binding teaching—that is, it need not be accepted by practicing Catholics, though they must give it thoughtful and respectful consideration. It would be remarkable to think otherwise—that a couple of paragraphs in an encyclical almost entirely devoted not to crime and punishment but to abortion and euthanasia was intended authoritatively to sweep aside (if one could) two thousand years of Christian teaching.

So I have given this new position thoughtful and careful consideration—and I disagree. That is not to say I favor the death penalty (I am judicially and judiciously neutral on that point); it is only to say that I do not find the death penalty immoral. I am happy to have reached that conclusion, because I like my job, and would rather not resign. And I am happy because I do not think it would be a good thing if American Catholics running for legislative office had to oppose the death penalty (most of them would not be elected); if American Catholics running for governor had to promise commutation of all death sentences (most of them would never reach the governor's mansion); if American Catholics were ineligible to go on the bench in all jurisdictions imposing the death penalty; or if American Catholics were subject to recusal when called for jury duty in capital cases.

I find it ironic that the Church's new (albeit nonbinding) position on the death penalty—which, if accepted, would have these *disastrous* consequences—is said to rest upon "prudential considerations." Is it prudent, when one is not certain enough about the point to proclaim it in a binding manner (and with good reason, given the long and consistent Christian tradition to the contrary), to effectively urge the retirement of Catholics from public life in a country where the federal government and thirty-eight of the states (comprising about 85 percent of the population) believe the death penalty is sometimes just and appropriate? Is it prudent to imperil acceptance of the Church's hard but traditional teachings on birth control and abortion and euthanasia (teachings that *have been* proclaimed in a binding manner, a distinction that the average Catholic layman is unlikely to grasp) by packaging them—under the wrapper "respect for life"—with another uncongenial doctrine *that everyone knows does not represent the traditional Christian view*? Perhaps, one is invited to conclude, all four of them are recently made up. We need some new staffers at the Congregation of Prudence in the Vatican. At least the new doctrine should have been urged only upon secular Europe, where it is at home.

Conscience and the Constitution—from *Employment Division v. Smith*

The First Amendment to the Constitution states that "Congress shall make no law respecting an establishment of religion, or prohibiting the free exercise thereof." These dual guarantees, known as the Establishment Clause and the Free Exercise Clause, have been deemed by the Supreme Court to apply against the states as well as the federal government. Their meaning has been the subject of extensive disputes.

Justice Scalia's majority opinion on the Free Exercise Clause in Employment Division v. Smith *(1990) is surely his most controversial opinion among supporters of religious liberty. Here is how the case arose: Alfred Smith and Galen Black, members of the Native American Church, ingested the psychoactive substance peyote for sacramental purposes. Their possession of peyote violated Oregon law. They were fired from their jobs with a private drug-rehabilitation organization as a result, and they were also determined to be ineligible for unemployment benefits because they had been fired for work-related misconduct. An Oregon court reversed that determination on the ground that the denial of benefits violated their rights under the Free Exercise Clause.*

In his majority opinion, Justice Scalia held that a "neutral law of general applicability" does not violate the Free Exercise

*Clause even if it heavily burdens a person's exercise of religion.
Oregon banned possession of peyote as part of its general criminal prohibition on possession of controlled substances. That ban
therefore did not violate Smith's and Black's rights under the
Free Exercise Clause, even though it prevented their sacramental use of peyote.*

*Justice Scalia rejected an alternative test under which gov-
ernmental actions that substantially burden a religious practice
would have to be justified by a compelling governmental interest. Any society that adopted and faithfully applied such a test
would, he argued, make each conscience "a law unto itself" and
thus be "courting anarchy." Exemptions protective of religious
liberty are matters for the political process, not for the courts.
(In the aftermath of the Court's ruling, Oregon enacted an exemption for religious use of peyote.)*

This case requires us to decide whether the Free Exercise Clause of the First Amendment permits the State
of Oregon to include religiously inspired peyote use
within the reach of its general criminal prohibition on
use of that drug, and thus permits the State to deny
unemployment benefits to persons dismissed from
their jobs because of such religiously inspired use.

The Free Exercise Clause of the First Amendment,
which has been made applicable to the States by incor-
poration into the Fourteenth Amendment, provides
that "Congress shall make no law respecting an establishment of religion, or *prohibiting the free exercise
thereof. . . .*" The free exercise of religion means, first

and foremost, the right to believe and profess whatever religious doctrine one desires. Thus, the First Amendment obviously excludes all "governmental regulation of religious beliefs as such." The government may not compel affirmation of religious belief, punish the expression of religious doctrines it believes to be false, impose special disabilities on the basis of religious views or religious status, or lend its power to one or the other side in controversies over religious authority or dogma.

But the "exercise of religion" often involves not only belief and profession but the performance of (or abstention from) physical acts: assembling with others for a worship service, participating in sacramental use of bread and wine, proselytizing, abstaining from certain foods or certain modes of transportation. It would be true, we think (though no case of ours has involved the point), that a state would be "prohibiting the free exercise [of religion]" if it sought to ban such acts or abstentions only when they are engaged in for religious reasons, or only because of the religious belief that they display. It would doubtless be unconstitutional, for example, to ban the casting of "statues that are to be used for worship purposes," or to prohibit bowing down before a golden calf.

[Smith and Black], however, seek to carry the meaning of "prohibiting the free exercise [of religion]" one large step further. They contend that their religious motivation for using peyote places them beyond the reach of a criminal law that is not specifically directed at their religious practice, and that is concededly constitutional as applied to those who use the drug for other reasons. They assert, in other words, that "prohibiting the free exercise [of religion]" includes requiring any individual to observe a generally applicable law that requires (or forbids) the performance of an act that his religious belief forbids (or requires). As a textual matter, we do not think the words must be given that meaning. It is no more necessary to regard the collection of a general tax, for example, as "prohibiting the free exercise [of religion]" by those citizens who believe support of organized government to be sinful than it is to regard the same tax as "abridging the freedom . . . of the press" of those publishing companies that must pay the tax as a condition of staying in business. It is a permissible reading of the text, in the one case as in the other, to say that, if prohibiting the exercise of religion (or burdening the activity of printing) is not the object of the tax, but merely the incidental effect of a generally applicable and otherwise valid provision, the First Amendment has not been offended.

Our decisions reveal that the latter reading is the correct one. We have never held that an individual's religious beliefs excuse him from compliance with an otherwise valid law prohibiting conduct that the State is free to regulate. On the contrary, the record of more than a century of our free-exercise jurisprudence contradicts that proposition. As described succinctly by Justice Frankfurter in *Minersville School District Board of Education v. Gobitis* (1940):

> Conscientious scruples have not, in the course of the long struggle for religious toleration, relieved the individual from obedience to a general law not aimed at the promotion or restriction of religious beliefs. The mere possession of religious convictions which contradict the relevant concerns of a political society does not relieve the citizen from the discharge of political responsibilities.

We first had occasion to assert that principle in *Reynolds v. United States* (1879), where we rejected the claim that criminal laws against polygamy could not be constitutionally applied to those whose religion commanded the practice. "Laws," we said,

> are made for the government of actions, and while they cannot interfere with mere religious belief and opinions, they may with practices. Can a man excuse his practices to the contrary because of his religious belief? To permit this would be to make the professed doctrines of religious belief superior to the law of the land, and in effect to permit every citizen to become a law unto himself.

Subsequent decisions have consistently held that the right of free exercise does not relieve an individual of the obligation to comply with a valid and neutral law of general applicability on the ground that the law proscribes (or prescribes) conduct that his religion prescribes (or proscribes).

[Smith and Black] urge us to hold, quite simply, that when otherwise prohibitable conduct is accompanied by religious convictions, not only the convictions but the conduct itself must be free from governmental regulation. We have never held that, and decline to do so now. There being no contention that Oregon's drug law represents an attempt to regulate religious beliefs, the communication of religious beliefs, or the raising of one's children in those beliefs, the rule to which we have adhered ever since *Reynolds* plainly controls.

The government's ability to enforce generally applicable prohibitions of socially harmful conduct, like its ability to carry out other aspects of public policy, "cannot depend on measuring the effects of a governmental action on a religious objector's spiritual development" [citation omitted]. To make an individual's obligation to obey such a law contingent upon the law's coincidence with his religious beliefs, except where the State's interest is "compelling"—permitting him, by virtue of his beliefs, "to become a law unto himself"—contradicts both constitutional tradition and common sense.

The "compelling government interest" requirement

seems benign, because it is familiar from other fields. But using it as the standard that must be met before the government may accord different treatment on the basis of race, or before the government may regulate the content of speech, is not remotely comparable to using it for the purpose asserted here. What it produces in those other fields—equality of treatment, and an unrestricted flow of contending speech—are constitutional norms; what it would produce here—a private right to ignore generally applicable laws—is a constitutional anomaly.

Nor is it possible to limit the impact of [their] proposal by requiring a "compelling state interest" only when the conduct prohibited is "central" to the individual's religion. It is no more appropriate for judges to determine the "centrality" of religious beliefs before applying a "compelling interest" test in the free-exercise field than it would be for them to determine the "importance" of ideas before applying the "compelling interest" test in the free speech field. What principle of law or logic can be brought to bear to contradict a believer's assertion that a particular act is "central" to his personal faith? Judging the centrality of different religious practices is akin to the unacceptable "business of evaluating the relative merits of differing religious claims" [citation omitted]. As we reaffirmed only last term, "it is not within the judicial ken to question the centrality of particular beliefs or practices to a faith, or the validity of particular litigants' interpretation of those creeds."

If the "compelling interest" test is to be applied at all, then, it must be applied across the board, to all actions thought to be religiously commanded. Moreover, if "compelling interest" really means what it says (and watering it down here would subvert its rigor in the other fields where it is applied), many laws will not meet the test. Any society adopting such a system would be courting anarchy, but that danger increases in direct proportion to the society's diversity of religious beliefs, and its determination to coerce or suppress none of them. Precisely because "we are a cosmopolitan nation made up of people of almost every conceivable religious preference" and precisely because we value and protect that religious divergence, we cannot afford the luxury of deeming *presumptively invalid*, as applied to the religious objector, every regulation of conduct that does not protect an interest of the highest order [citation omitted]. The rule [Smith and Black] favor would open the prospect of constitutionally required religious exemptions from civic obligations of almost every conceivable kind—ranging from compulsory military service, to the payment of taxes, to health and safety regulation such as manslaughter and child neglect laws, compulsory vaccination laws, drug laws, and traffic laws, to social welfare legislation such as minimum wage laws, child labor laws, animal cruelty laws, environmental protection laws, and laws providing for equality of opportunity for the races. The First Amendment's protection of religious liberty does not require this.

Values that are protected against government interference through enshrinement in the Bill of Rights are not thereby banished from the political process. Just as a society that believes in the negative protection accorded to the press by the First Amendment is likely to enact laws that affirmatively foster the dissemination of the printed word, so also a society that believes in the negative protection accorded to religious belief can be expected to be solicitous of that value in its legislation as well. It is therefore not surprising that a number of states have made an exception to their drug laws for sacramental peyote use. But to say that a nondiscriminatory religious practice exemption is permitted, or even that it is desirable, is not to say that it is constitutionally required, and that the appropriate occasions for its creation can be discerned by the courts. It may fairly be said that leaving accommodation to the political process will place at a relative disadvantage those religious practices that are not widely engaged in; but that unavoidable consequence of democratic government must be preferred to a system in which each conscience is a law unto itself or in which judges weigh the social importance of all laws against the centrality of all religious beliefs.

Absolute Standards of Conduct—Lessons from the Holocaust

In 1987 Justice Scalia delivered the principal address at the annual Days of Remembrance commemoration for victims of the Holocaust, held in the U.S. Capitol Rotunda. Reflecting on this "tale of insanity and diabolical cruelty," he argued that the Holocaust should remind us that even the most sophisticated civilizations are capable of unimaginable evil. To prevent a recurrence of such horror, he urged that "we re-dedicate ourselves" to the "absolute, uncompromisable standards of human conduct" set forth in the Ten Commandments.

Distinguished members of the United States Senate and House of Representatives; members of the diplomatic corps; survivors of the Holocaust; ladies and gentlemen:

I was profoundly honored to have been invited to speak at this annual ceremony in remembrance of those consumed in the Holocaust. But it is not, I must tell you, an easy assignment for a non-Jew to undertake. I am an outsider speaking to an ancient people about a tragedy of unimaginable proportions that is intensely personal to them. I have no memories of parents or children, uncles or cousins caught up in and destroyed by the horror. I have not even that distinctive appreciation of evil that must come from knowing that six million people were killed for no other reason than that they had blood like mine running in their veins.

More difficult still, I am not only not a Jew, but I am a Christian, and I know that the anti-Semitism of many of my uncomprehending co-religionists, over many centuries, helped set the stage for the mad tragedy that the National Socialists produced. I say uncomprehending co-religionists, not only because my religion teaches that it is wrong to hate anyone, but because it is particularly absurd for a Christian to hate the people of Israel. That is to hate one's spiritual parents, and to sever one's roots.

When I was a young man in college, spending my junior year abroad, I saw Dachau. Later, in the year after I graduated from law school, I saw Auschwitz. I will of course never forget the impression they made upon me. If some playwright or novelist had invented such a tale of insanity and diabolical cruelty, it would not be believed. But it did happen. The one message I want to convey today is that you will have missed the most frightening aspect of it all, if you do not appreciate that it happened in one of the most educated, most progressive, most cultured countries in the world.

The Germany of the late 1920s and early 1930s was a world leader in most fields of art, science, and intellect. Berlin was a center of theater; with the assistance of the famous producer Max Reinhardt, playwrights and composers of the caliber of Bertolt Brecht and Kurt Weill flourished. Berlin had three opera houses, and Germany as a whole no less than eighty. Every middle-sized city had its own orchestra. German poets and writers included Hermann Hesse, Stefan George, Leonhard Frank, Franz Kafka, and Thomas Mann, who won the Nobel Prize for Literature in 1929. In architecture, Germany was the cutting edge, with Gropius and the Bauhaus school. It boasted painters like Paul Klee and Oskar Schlemmer. Musical composers like Anton Webern, Alban Berg, Arnold Schoenberg, and Paul Hindemith. Conductors like Otto Klemperer, Bruno Walter, Erich Kleiber, and Wilhelm Furtwängler. And in science, of course, the Germans were preeminent. To quote a recent article in the *Journal of the American Medical Association*:

> In 1933, when the National Socialist Party came to power in Germany, the biomedical enterprise in that country was among the most sophisticated in the world. German contributions to biochemistry, physiology, medicine, surgery, and public health, as well as to clinical training, had shaped to an important degree the academic and practice patterns of the time, and clinical training and research experience in the great German clinics and laboratories had been widely sought for decades by physicians and basic scientists from around the world.

To fully grasp the horror of the Holocaust, you must imagine (for it probably happened) that the commandant of Auschwitz or Dachau, when he had finished his day's work, retired to his apartment to eat a meal that was in the finest good taste, and then to listen, perhaps, to some tender and poignant *lieder* of Franz Schubert.

This aspect of the matter is perhaps so prominent in my mind because I am undergoing, currently, the task of selecting a college for the youngest of my children—or perhaps more accurately, trying to help her select it. How much stock we place in education, intellect, cultural refinement! And how much of our substance we are prepared to expend to give our children the very best opportunity to acquire education, intellect, cultural refinement! Yet those qualities are of only secondary importance—to our children, and to the society that their generation will create. I am reminded of words written by John Henry Newman long before the Holocaust could even be imagined.

> Knowledge is one thing, virtue is another; good sense is not conscience, refinement is not humility. Liberal Education makes the gentleman. It is well to be a gentleman, it is well to have a cultivated intellect, a delicate taste, a candid, equitable, dispassionate mind, a noble and courteous bearing in the conduct of life. These are the connatural qualities of a large knowledge; they are the objects of a university. But they are no guar-

antee for sanctity or even for conscientiousness; they may attach to the man of the world, to the profligate, to the heartless.

Yes, to the heartless.

It is the purpose of these annual Holocaust remembrances—as it is the purpose of the nearby Holocaust museum—not only to honor the memory of the six million Jews and three or four million other poor souls caught up in this twentieth-century terror, but also, by keeping the memory of their tragedy painfully alive, to prevent its happening again. The latter can be achieved only by acknowledging, and passing on to our children, the existence of absolute, uncompromisable standards of human conduct. Mankind has traditionally derived such standards from religion; and the West has derived them from and through the Jews. Those absolute and uncompromisable standards of human conduct will not endure without an effort to make them endure, and it is to that enterprise that we re-dedicate ourselves today. They are in the Decalogue, and they are in the question put and answered by Micah: "What doth the Lord require of thee, but to do justly, to love mercy, and to walk humbly with thy God?"

For those six million Jews to whom it was not done justly, who were shown no mercy, and for whom God and his laws were abandoned: may we remember their sufferings, and may they rest in peace.

The Talmudic Justice

BY RABBI MEIR SOLOVEICHIK

Were all reeds quills, and all mankind scribes, they would not suffice to write the Torah that I have learned, even though I abstracted from it no more than a man would take by dipping the tip of his painting stick into the sea.

—Rabbi Joshua, the Talmud

A Talmudic maxim instructs with respect to the Scripture: "Turn it over, and turn it over, for all is therein." Divinely inspired text may contain the answers to all earthly questions, but the Due Process Clause most assuredly does not.

—Antonin Scalia, dissent in
Caperton v. A.T. Massey Coal Co. (2009)

Several years ago, I had the honor of hosting Justice Scalia at Yeshiva University with his longtime friend Nathan Lewin. In the private event before our public discussion, I took note of the fact that he was the only justice on the Court—at least in recent memory—to have cited the Talmud, and that his Jewish colleagues, through long and distinguished careers, failed to do so. This, I concluded, was ample reason to award Justice Scalia the title of the "Talmudic Justice." I believe the justice was tickled by the idea. It was one of many memorable moments in an unforgettable day.

Thinking it over, now that he is gone, I do indeed believe that the appellation Talmudic Justice is an apt one. Justice Scalia was an admirer of those who ably engaged in eloquent argumentation, and the rabbis of the Talmud are practitioners par excellence of this art.

The justice appreciated brilliance, and the vastness of the Talmud testifies to the capacity of the human mind.

Yet as the great Talmudist Rabbi Joseph Soloveitchik has noted, the rabbis of the Talmud, their brilliance notwithstanding, leave many questions unresolved, for answers to be revealed in times to come. This meant, to utilize a phrase of which Rabbi Soloveitchik was fond, that the geniuses of the Talmud embodied simultaneously legal "majesty and humility." Strikingly, the rabbinic aphorism cited by Scalia about the Torah—"turn it over, for all is in it"—was said by one of the least famous rabbis in the Talmud, who believed, as did his colleagues, that the Word of God may contain all the answers, but no one man can discover them all. True intellectual greatness—epitomized by the great Rabbi Joshua's statement cited above—lies in recognition of one's gifts but also of one's utter lack of omniscience.

If humility is essential for authorized interpreters

of the word of God, then it is all the more necessary for judges in a democracy, and this insight lay at the heart of the worldview of the man whose faith we celebrate in this book. Scalia understood—and spent decades eloquently attempting to persuade his colleagues and countrymen—that the greatness of the American Founders lay not only in their brilliance, but in their understanding that no individual, no matter how brilliant, could resolve all moral and political questions for future generations. Words of the justice written when I was a teenager are seared into my memory and helped make me an originalist: "To counterbalance the Court's criticism of our ancestors," he wrote in dissent in the VMI case (*United States v. Virginia*, 1996), "let me say a word in their praise: They left us free to change. The same cannot be said of this most illiberal Court." Justice Scalia did not lack confidence, but he taught us that for a judge to assume that he or she has all the answers is both arrogant and undemocratic.

"The beginning of wisdom is the fear of the Lord," we are instructed by the Bible. True wisdom lies in our recognition of our intellectual talents and limitations and in our recognition that there is only One Who has all the answers. Justice Scalia understood this all too well; and for all that he valued intelligence, he also recognized that brilliance and goodness do not necessarily go hand in hand. This is the essential message of the moving description of his visit to Dachau as a college student and his warning about the lesson of the Holocaust: "The one message I want to convey today is that you will have missed the most frightening aspect of it all, if you do not appreciate that it happened in one of the most educated, most progressive, most cultured countries in the world."

Scalia's quotation of Cardinal Newman is particularly apt: "Knowledge is one thing, virtue is another; good sense is not conscience, refinement is not humility." To read Scalia's opinions following his passing is to miss his brilliance; but to ponder the faithful perspective of the Talmudic Justice is to miss something even more invaluable: his wisdom.

Rabbi Meir Soloveichik is the director of the Straus Center for Torah and Western Thought at Yeshiva University.

"O tempora! O mores!"

BY KRISTIN A. LINSLEY

I never expected that Justice Scalia would influence me on matters of faith. During my clerkship, the issue of personal faith was rarely if ever discussed. It certainly never entered into our discussions of cases—even those, such as *Employment Division v. Smith*, that involved the religion clauses of the Constitution. Justice Scalia approached these cases as he did any others, by reference to the text and history of the relevant constitutional provisions.

But later, I came to appreciate the justice's faith through other means. My own spiritual path had led me to Catholicism, so this became yet another reason to engage with Justice Scalia. Having learned from him on matters of legal meaning, I began to understand the depth and breadth of his faith—and the fact that he brought the same intellectual passion and discipline to such matters as he did to legal issues. And although his faith never affected his judicial reasoning, there *were* certain parallels—most notably, the centrality of text within its appropriate hierarchy; a deep intellectual tradition; a belief in right and wrong, and in the

existence of objective truth; and the richness and rel-
evance of historical tradition. The strength of Justice
Scalia's faith, like that of his intellect and legal vision,
was profoundly humbling to me and to others who engaged him on that topic.

Justice Scalia never set aside his sense of humor and
perspective, and that was true on matters of faith as
well. The day I joined the Catholic Church, I emailed
him to thank him for his support during the process
and to say that I was happy to be joining his Church.
"Not mine," he wrote back. "Christ's. I and the rest of
us sinners welcome you." He then shared a story of a
funeral he'd attended earlier that week at Arlington
National Cemetery. The deceased had served in World
War II and the Korean War and risen to the rank of
major general, and the justice noted that it was a "big
funeral—caisson with white horses, twenty-one-gun
salute, the whole megillah." The priest told the assembled group that the deceased was in heaven now, and
that everyone could pray to him. But that did not fool
the man's "good ol' Chicago Irish-Catholic family." The
justice said he told a relative afterward that he would
pray for the deceased's miserable soul, as he hoped
someone would pray for his when he was gone. She said
she could not agree more, and that the family members were staring at one another in disbelief when the
priest announced the man's sainthood. "O tempora! O
mores!" the justice concluded.

The justice always knew that his life on earth could
end in an instant, without warning—"Poof, it's gone,"

he would say. His faith taught him to be prepared for that moment. It was his job to be ready when the time came, and, if he was ready, he and others had no need to fear.

Although I miss Justice Scalia greatly, I take comfort in the knowledge that his deep and abiding faith will guide him from here.

Kristin A. Linsley practices law in San Francisco. She clerked for Justice Scalia during the Court's October 1989 term.

Latin and Greek

BY FATHER ROBERT CONNOR

I took a leave of absence from Marquette Medical School in the spring of 1958 after my freshman year for the purpose of going to Rome nine months later. I had joined Opus Dei the previous February and was offered the opportunity to be in Rome with the founder, Saint Josemaría Escrivá, and to pursue studies in philosophy and theology while there. While life-changing, the right choice was clear to me. My mother, though, was beside herself.

As the date approached for me to leave for Rome, she pulled out all the stops. She went to the headmaster of my high school, whom she knew well, and also to a young man who was famous in my house: Antonin Scalia. My parents had come to admire Nino through my close friendship with him; my father had been especially impressed when Nino, during a televised high school debate, "cross-examined" guest panelist Averell Harriman, who was director of the Mutual Security Agency at the time and went on to become governor of New York.

Scalia and I had spent four years at Xavier High

School, 1949 to 1953, studying in the same home-room and taking the same classes. We did four years of Latin and three of Greek, and found ourselves duly exercised—particularly in Latin—in our junior year when our instructor drove us relentlessly through the five declensions of nouns and four conjugations of verbs under pressure of a stopwatch. We were marked on speed and accuracy every morning. This was followed by approximately thirty lines of Cicero's *Catiline Orations* to translate, then turning an English sentence into Latin, with all the pitfalls of verb complexities. Daunting work. Every day. Through the misery, we got to be good friends. After coming into contact again in 1983, there was not a time that we saw each other and did not revel in the conjugation of some irregular verb or laugh with the sheer joy of reciting the conjugations by rote, pulling them out of some recondite cavity of memory we both had within.

At my mother's bidding, Scalia and Father John J. Morrison appeared at my house in Jamaica, Queens, in June 1959. The priest tried to give me a sense of timing and proportion, which I thanked him for. Nino asked what this was all about. I explained Opus Dei as I understood it, and the imperative I experienced to give it all—now—in this radical way of being in the world and living Christ. He took in everything I said and got it: "Sounds good to me." I don't know what he said to my mother on the way out, but it was decisive. He had the stature and authority, even then, to calm nerves. I appreciated that he took the time and effort to do what he did, and seeing it now in the perspective of who he was, I love him for it. What was astounding to me over the years was his loyalty to that friendship built on a few Latin and Greek verbs.

Father Robert Connor is a numerary priest with Opus Dei and the chaplain of the Southmont Center in South Orange, New Jersey. (A version of this recollection was previously published in National Review, *which has given its permission to publish this recollection.)*

PART III

PUBLIC LESSONS
FOR AMERICANS

A Nation Under God—Public Expressions of Faith

Our country has a long tradition of official encouragement of religion on a non-sectarian basis. That tradition reflects the understanding of the nation's founders that, as George Washington declared in his Farewell Address, religion and morality are "indispensable supports" of "political prosperity" and that we should "with caution indulge the supposition that morality can be maintained without religion."

Speaking at a Marine Corps air station's prayer breakfast in 1998, Justice Scalia celebrated our traditional belief, expressed unashamedly in our national pronouncements and reflected faithfully in our public policies, that we are a nation under God.

I want to speak to you this morning about tradition. The Marine Corps understands the value of that elusive, intangible quality. It is there in your motto: Always Faithful. Not just faithful today; not just faithful from now on; but faithful always, from 1775 to the present, and for as long as the republic will call upon you. It is there in the "Marines' Hymn," which recalls expeditions against enemies of the republic so long gone and so long forgotten that few Americans, alas, even know what the Halls of Montezuma were. And it is there, of course, in your battle pendants, giving witness to a long road of fidelity and honor from Tripoli to Iwo Jima to Iraq.

It is a strange thing, tradition. It can be squandered, but not bought. It can be lost, but not given to someone else. In the field of human activity in which I toil—the law—the newly emerged democracies of Eastern Europe are trying to establish independent judiciaries, and we are trying to help them. But to tell you the truth, we cannot help them very much. We can tell them of our two-century-long tradition of proud judicial independence, and urge them to emulate it. But we cannot *give* them a tradition of independence to replace their own lengthy traditions of judicial subservience to political authority. When we think "judge," we think of an impartial arbiter between the power of the state and the rights of the citizen; when they think "judge," they think of one of the faithful instruments of state power.

Because human institutions succeed or fail in large part because of the good traditions or the bad traditions that animate them—and because good traditions, once lost, are difficult if not impossible to re-establish—we must guard and nourish all of our valuable traditions with the same care and devotion that the Corps devotes to *Semper Fidelis*. I want to speak this morning about one of our oldest and I think most important national traditions that has for some years been in grave and imminent peril: the traditional belief, expressed unashamedly in our national pronouncements and reflected faithfully in our public policies, that we are a nation under God. That tradition appears, of course, in the first document to issue from us as a nation. The Declaration of Independence, which appeals to the "Laws of Nature, and of Nature's God," affirms that "all men . . . are endowed by their Creator with certain unalienable Rights," and asserts in its concluding sentence "a firm reliance on the protection of divine Providence." The first Congress to be elected under the new Constitution adopted a joint resolution requesting the president to "recommend to the people of the United States a day of public thanksgiving and prayer." President Washington responded to that request by issuing the first Thanksgiving Day proclamation, and of course we have had Thanksgiving Day proclamations ever since. We have also had, from the very beginning, publicly supported army and navy chaplains, House and Senate chaplains who open each day's sessions with a prayer, exemptions from state property taxes for houses of worship, "In God We Trust" on the coinage (since the Civil War), and yes, even opening of the sessions of the Supreme Court with the invocation "God save the United States and this Honorable Court."

This religious tradition of ours has consistently affirmed a national belief in God—but not a national belief in a particular religion. That has been the key distinction: between official encouragement of religion, which was always practiced, and official favoritism of particular religious sects, which was prohibited. The best exemplar of this distinctively American approach toward church and state was the greatest American of them all, the indispensable man, your first commander in chief, George Washington. When he presided over the 1787 convention in Philadelphia that drafted the Constitution, Washington wrote home to his wife, Martha, that "this morning, I attended the Popish mass." Imagine this aristocratic Virginian attending a Roman Catholic church service. He attended, of course, in his capacity as the virtual personification of the new nation that was in the process of forming; everyone knew he would be elected president, if the Constitution-drafting project were ever a success. And he attended to demonstrate that this new nation would not favor one sect over another. This was the same extraordinary man who, in the first year of his presidency, would write a letter addressed "To the Hebrew Congregation in Newport, Rhode Island," thanking them for their letter to him and saying among other things the following:

> It is now no more that toleration is spoken of, as
> if it was by the indulgence of one class of people,
> that another enjoyed the exercise of their inherent
> natural rights. For happily the Government of the
> United States, which gives to bigotry no sanction, to
> persecution no assistance requires only that they who
> live under its protection should demean themselves

as good citizens, in giving it on all occasions their
effectual support.

He concludes the letter:

May the children of the Stock of Abraham, who dwell
in this land, continue to merit and enjoy the good will
of the other inhabitants, while everyone shall sit in
safety under his own vine and fig tree, and there shall
be none to make him afraid.

May the Father of all mercies scatter light and not
darkness in our paths, and make us all in our several
vocations useful here, and in his own due time and
way everlastingly happy.

This long American tradition of official encouragement of religion, but strict neutrality among religious
sects, was acknowledged by my Court as recently as
1952. In a case upholding New York City's so-called
released-time program, whereby public-school children whose parents so requested were released from
school early one day each week so that they might attend religious instruction programs at their churches
or synagogues, the Supreme Court said the following:

We are a religious people whose institutions
presuppose a Supreme Being. When the state
encourages religious instruction or cooper-
ates with religious authorities by adjusting the
schedule of public events to sectarian needs, it

follows the best of our traditions. For it then respects the religious nature of our people and accommodates the public service to their spiritual
needs. The government must be neutral when it
comes to competition between sects. It may not
coerce anyone to attend church, to observe a religious holiday, or to take religious instruction.
But it can close its doors or suspend its operations as to those who want to repair to their religious sanctuary for worship or instruction.

That opinion for the Court was written, by the way,
by William O. Douglas, hardly one of the more conservative justices.

Why, then, do I say that our national tradition of
public religiousness is imperiled? Because many people, particularly opinion leaders, no longer believe
what Justice Douglas wrote, but rather espouse the
view that the government must be scrupulously impartial, not merely as between various religious sects
and denominations, but even as between religion in
general and atheism. The Constitution, these people
believe, forbids government from bestowing any special favor upon religion, even if it is done in a non-
sectarian fashion. How serious the situation is may
become apparent when I tell you that these people include (insofar as one can tell from the cases) a majority
of the justices of the Supreme Court. For the Court has
explicitly abandoned Justice Douglas's approach and

has demanded a scrupulously secular state. In a 1968 opinion, for example, the Court said the following:

> Government in our democracy, state and national, must be neutral in matters of religious theory, doctrine, and practice. The First Amendment mandates governmental neutrality between religion and religion, and between religion and nonreligion.

That position—mandated neutrality between religion and non-religion—is where the Court's jurisprudence in theory remains today. It was the basis, for example, for the Court's striking down in 1989 a Texas statute (which had counterparts in the laws of many other states) that exempted from state sales tax the sales of doctrinal religious publications—Bibles, Korans, and Talmuds. It was unconstitutional, the Court held, thus to favor religious belief.

I dissented from that opinion, because I do not believe in the principle of neutrality between religion and non-religion on which it is based. Indeed, it seems to me that the First Amendment itself is a repudiation of that principle, since the Free Exercise Clause gives special favor to the free exercise of religion. The neutrality principle is also contradicted by the many national practices, dating back to the earliest times, which I have described earlier.

The Court has changed its position on this matter

once—and hopefully will change it back once again. Indeed, to put it that way makes the Court's current jurisprudence sound much more logical than it in fact is—since the Court has continued to approve practices that are flatly inconsistent with the new principle of "neutrality between religion and nonreligion." It has approved, for example, the longstanding practice of legislative chaplains who open sessions of both state and federal legislatures with non-denominational prayers. And it has approved property-tax exemptions for church property. If you can figure out how these holdings are consistent with the principle that religion in general cannot be favored, you are sharper than I am.

If I were you, I would not look to Supreme Court opinions to figure out our national tradition on matters of this sort. A good person to look to, in this as in many other matters, is your first commander in chief. I will conclude with a few of his more prominent pronouncements, and you can judge for yourself whether he thought we somehow had to suppress the notion that we were a nation under God.

On November 2, 1783, at Rocky Hill, near Princeton, New Jersey, Washington issued his Farewell Orders to the bulk of the armies of the United States, which the Continental Congress had released from federal service. In the concluding paragraph of those orders he offered to the departing troops "his recommendations to their grateful country, and his prayers to the God of Armies. May ample justice be done them here, and may the choicest of heaven's favours, both here and hereafter, attend those who, under divine auspices, have secured innumerable blessings for others." About a month and a half later, on December 23, Washington addressed the Continental Congress at Annapolis on resigning his commission. The next-to-last sentence of his brief address was this: "I consider it an indispensable duty to close this last solemn act of my Official life, by commending the Interests of our dearest Country to the protection of Almighty God, and those who have the superintendence of them, to his holy keeping." One of the congressmen present reported that as he spoke the words "our dearest Country to the protection of Almighty God," his voice "faltered and sank and the whole house felt his agitations." He rode on horseback that day for Mount Vernon; he came up the driveway lined by trees that he had planted, Martha standing in the doorway, on Christmas Eve.

Washington left us another famous Farewell Address, the one he gave to all the citizens of the republic on September 19, 1796, when he advised them of his resolution not to stand for a third term as president. That lengthy address had something quite specific to say about his view of the relationship between religion and politics:

> Of all the dispositions and habits which lead to political prosperity, Religion and morality are indispensable supports. In vain would that man claim the tribute of Patriotism, who

should labour to subvert these great Pillars of human happiness, these firmest props of the duties of Men and citizens. The mere Politician, equally with the pious man ought to respect and to cherish them. A volume could not trace all their connections with private and public felicity. Let it simply be asked where is the security for property, for reputation, for life, if the sense of religious obligation *desert* the oaths, which are the instruments of investigation in Courts of Justice? And let us with caution indulge the supposition, that morality can be maintained without religion. Whatever may be conceded to the influence of refined education on minds of peculiar structure, reason and experience both forbid us to expect that National morality can prevail in exclusion of religious principle.

Finally, as a stellar example of what I mean by the religious faith central to our American political tradition, and also as the most appropriate conclusion imaginable to this prayer breakfast, let me read President Washington's and the nation's first Thanksgiving proclamation, issued in New York City on October 3, 1789:

Whereas it is the duty of all Nations to acknowledge the providence of Almighty God, to obey his will, to be grateful for his benefits, and humbly to implore his protection and favor—and whereas both Houses of Congress have by their joint Committee requested me "to recommend to the People of the United States a day of public thanksgiving and prayer to be observed by acknowledging with grateful hearts the many signal favors of Almighty God especially by affording them an opportunity peaceably to establish a form of government for their safety and happiness."

Now therefore I do recommend and assign Thursday the 26th day of November next to be devoted by the People of these States to the service of that great and glorious Being, who is the beneficent Author of all the good that was, that is, or that will be—That we may then all unite in rendering unto him our sincere and humble thanks—for his kind care and protection of the People of this Country previous to their becoming a Nation—for the signal and manifold mercies, and the favorable interpositions of his Providence which we experienced in the course and conclusion of the late war—for the great degree of tranquillity, union, and plenty which we have since enjoyed—for the peaceable and rational manner, in which we have been enabled to establish constitutions of government for our safety and happiness, and particularly the national One now lately instituted—for the civil and religious liberty with which we are blessed; and the means we have of acquiring and diffusing useful knowledge; and in general for all the great and various favors which he hath been pleased to confer upon us.

And also that we may then unite in most humbly offering our prayers and supplications to the great Lord and Ruler of Nations and beseech Him to pardon our national and other transgressions—to enable us all, whether in public or private stations, to perform our several and relative duties properly and punctually—to render our national government a blessing to all the people, by constantly being a Government of wise, just, and constitutional laws, discreetly and faithfully executed and obeyed—to protect and guide all Sovereigns and Nations (especially such as have shewn kindness unto us) and to bless them with good government, peace, and concord—to promote the knowledge and practice of true religion and virtue, and the encrease of science among them and us—and generally to grant unto all Mankind such a degree of temporal prosperity as he alone knows to be best.

Publicly Honoring the Ten Commandments— from *McCreary County v. ACLU*

The First Amendment's Establishment Clause prohibits laws "respecting an establishment of religion." In McCreary County v. ACLU *(2005), the Supreme Court ruled by a 5–4 vote that displays of the Ten Commandments in courthouses in two Kentucky counties violated the Establishment Clause. In his dissent, Justice Scalia argued that the majority's core premise—that the Establishment Clause mandates government neutrality between religion and non-religion—is alien to the American model of the relationship between church and state: "Those who wrote the Constitution believed that morality was essential to the well-being of society and that encouragement of religion was the best way to foster morality."*

On September 11, 2001, I was attending in Rome, Italy, an international conference of judges and lawyers, principally from Europe and the United States. That night and the next morning virtually all of the participants watched, in their hotel rooms, the address to the nation by the president of the United States concerning the murderous attacks upon the Twin Towers and the Pentagon, in which thousands of Americans had been killed. The address ended, as presidential addresses often do, with the prayer "God bless America." The next afternoon I was approached by one of the judges from a European country, who, after extending his profound condolences for my country's loss, sadly observed, "How I wish that the head of state of my country, at a similar time of national tragedy and distress, could conclude his address 'God bless _____.' It is of course absolutely forbidden."

That is one model of the relationship between church and state—a model spread across Europe by the armies of Napoleon, and reflected in the Constitution of France, which begins, "France is [a] . . . secular . . . Republic." Religion is to be strictly excluded from the public forum. This is not, and never was, the model adopted by America. George Washington added to the form of presidential oath prescribed by the Constitution the concluding words "so help me God." The Supreme Court under John Marshall opened its sessions with the prayer "God save the United States and this Honorable Court." The First Congress instituted the practice of beginning its legislative sessions with a prayer. The same week that Congress submitted the Establishment Clause as part of the Bill of Rights for ratification by the states, it enacted legislation providing for paid chaplains in the House and Senate. The day after the First Amendment was proposed, the same Congress that had proposed it requested the president to proclaim "a day of public thanksgiving and prayer, to be observed, by acknowledging, with grateful

hearts, the many and signal favours of Almighty God."
President Washington offered the first Thanksgiving
Proclamation shortly thereafter, devoting November 26, 1789, on behalf of the American people "'to the
service of that great and glorious Being who is the beneficent author of all the good that is, that was, or that
will be,'" thus beginning a tradition of offering gratitude to God that continues today. The same Congress
also re-enacted the Northwest Territory Ordinance of
1787, Article III of which provided: "Religion, morality, and knowledge, being necessary to good government and the happiness of mankind, schools and the
means of education shall forever be encouraged." And
of course the First Amendment itself accords religion
(and no other manner of belief) special constitutional
protection.

These actions of our first president and Congress
and the Marshall Court were not idiosyncratic; they
reflected the beliefs of the period. Those who wrote
the Constitution believed that morality was essential
to the well-being of society and that encouragement
of religion was the best way to foster morality. The
"fact that the Founding Fathers believed devotedly
that there was a God and that the unalienable rights
of man were rooted in Him is clearly evidenced in their
writings, from the Mayflower Compact to the Constitution itself." [Quoting 1963 Supreme Court ruling.]
President Washington opened his presidency with a
prayer and reminded his fellow citizens at the conclusion of it that "reason and experience both forbid us to

expect that National morality can prevail in exclusion of religious principle." President John Adams wrote to the Massachusetts Militia: "We have no government armed with power capable of contending with human passions unbridled by morality and religion. Our Constitution was made only for a moral and religious people. It is wholly inadequate to the government of any other." Thomas Jefferson concluded his second inaugural address by inviting his audience to pray:

> I shall need, too, the favor of that Being in whose hands we are, who led our fathers, as Israel of old, from their native land and planted them in a country flowing with all the necessaries and comforts of life; who has covered our infancy with His providence and our riper years with His wisdom and power and to whose goodness I ask you to join in supplications with me that He will so enlighten the minds of your servants, guide their councils, and prosper their measures that whatsoever they do shall result in your good, and shall secure to you the peace, friendship, and approbation of all nations.

James Madison, in his first inaugural address, likewise placed his confidence "in the guardianship and guidance of that Almighty Being whose power regulates the destiny of nations, whose blessings have been so conspicuously dispensed to this rising Republic, and to whom we are bound to address our devout gratitude for the past, as well as our fervent supplications and best hopes for the future."

Nor have the views of our people on this matter significantly changed. Presidents continue to conclude the presidential oath with the words "so help me God." Our legislatures, state and national, continue to open their sessions with prayer led by official chaplains. The sessions of this Court continue to open with the prayer "God save the United States and this Honorable Court." Invocation of the Almighty by our public figures, at all levels of government, remains commonplace. Our coinage bears the motto "IN GOD WE TRUST." And our Pledge of Allegiance contains the acknowledgment that we are a nation "under God." As one of our Supreme Court opinions rightly observed, "We are a religious people whose institutions presuppose a Supreme Being."

With all of this reality (and much more) staring it in the face, how can the Court *possibly* assert that "'the First Amendment mandates governmental neutrality between . . . religion and nonreligion'" and that "[m]anifesting a purpose to favor . . . adherence to religion generally" is unconstitutional? Who says so? Surely not the words of the Constitution. Surely not the history and traditions that reflect our society's constant understanding of those words. Surely not even the current sense of our society, recently reflected in an act of Congress adopted *unanimously* by the Senate and with only five nays in the House of Representatives, criticizing a Court of Appeals opinion that had held "under

God" in the Pledge of Allegiance unconstitutional. Nothing stands behind the Court's assertion that governmental affirmation of the society's belief in God is unconstitutional except the Court's own say-so, citing as support only the unsubstantiated say-so of earlier Courts going back no farther than the mid-twentieth century. And it is, moreover, a thoroughly discredited say-so. It is discredited, to begin with, because a majority of the justices on the current Court (including at least one member of today's majority) have, in separate opinions, repudiated the brain-spun *"Lemon* test" that embodies the supposed principle of neutrality between religion and irreligion. And it is discredited because the Court has not had the courage (or the foolhardiness) to apply the neutrality principle consistently.

Besides appealing to the demonstrably false principle that the government cannot favor religion over irreligion, today's opinion suggests that the posting of the Ten Commandments violates the principle that the government cannot favor one religion over another. That is indeed a valid principle where public aid or assistance to religion is concerned, or where the free exercise of religion is at issue, but it necessarily applies in a more limited sense to public acknowledgment of the Creator. If religion in the public forum had to be entirely non-denominational, there could be no religion in the public forum at all. One cannot say the word "God" or "the Almighty," one cannot offer public supplication or thanksgiving, without contradicting the beliefs of some people that there are many gods, or that God or the gods pay no attention to human affairs. With respect to public acknowledgment of religious belief, it is entirely clear from our nation's historical practices that the Establishment Clause permits this disregard of polytheists and believers in unconcerned deities, just as it permits the disregard of devout atheists. The Thanksgiving Proclamation issued by George Washington at the instance of the First Congress was scrupulously non-denominational—but it was monotheistic. In *Marsh v. Chambers* (1983), we said that the fact the particular prayers offered in the Nebraska Legislature were "in the Judeo-Christian tradition" posed no additional problem, because "there is no indication that the prayer opportunity has been exploited to proselytize or advance any one, or to disparage any other, faith or belief."

Historical practices thus demonstrate that there is a distance between the acknowledgment of a single Creator and the establishment of a religion. The former is, as *Marsh v. Chambers* put it, "a tolerable acknowledgment of beliefs widely held among the people of this country." The three most popular religions in the United States, Christianity, Judaism, and Islam—which combined account for 97.7 percent of all believers—are monotheistic. All of them, moreover (Islam included), believe that the Ten Commandments were given by God to Moses, and are divine prescriptions for a virtuous life. Publicly honoring the Ten

Commandments is thus indistinguishable, insofar as discriminating against other religions is concerned, from publicly honoring God. Both practices are recognized across such a broad and diverse range of the population—from Christians to Muslims—that they cannot be reasonably understood as a government endorsement of a particular religious viewpoint.

Finally, I must respond to Justice Stevens's assertion that I would "marginalize the belief systems of more than seven million Americans" who adhere to religions that are not monotheistic. Surely that is a gross exaggeration. The beliefs of those citizens are entirely protected by the Free Exercise Clause, and by those aspects of the Establishment Clause that do not relate to government acknowledgment of the Creator. Invocation of God despite their beliefs is permitted not because non-monotheistic religions cease to be religions recognized by the religion clauses of the First Amendment, but because governmental invocation of God is not an establishment. Justice Stevens fails to recognize that in the context of public acknowledgments of God there are legitimate *competing* interests: on the one hand, the interest of that minority in not feeling "excluded"; but on the other, the interest of the overwhelming majority of religious believers in being able to give God thanks and supplication *as a people*, and with respect to our national endeavors. Our national tradition has resolved that conflict in favor of the majority. It is not for this Court to change a disposition that accounts, many Americans think, for the phenomenon remarked upon in a quotation attributed to various authors, including Bismarck, but which I prefer to associate with Charles de Gaulle: "God watches over little children, drunkards, and the United States of America."

The Right to Public Prayer— from *Lee v. Weisman*

In Lee v. Weisman *(1992), the Supreme Court ruled, by a 5–4 vote, that non-sectarian benedictions and invocations at public high school and middle school graduation ceremonies violate the Establishment Clause because the school district's control of the ceremonies "places public pressure, as well as peer pressure, on attending students to stand as a group or, at least, maintain respectful silence" during the prayers. In his dissent, Justice Scalia complained that the majority's "psychojourney" wandered far astray from the longstanding American tradition of non-sectarian prayer to God at public celebrations.*

In holding that the Establishment Clause prohibits invocations and benedictions at public school graduation ceremonies, the Court—with nary a mention that it is doing so—lays waste a tradition that is as old as public school graduation ceremonies themselves and that is a component of an even more longstanding American tradition of non-sectarian prayer to God at public celebrations generally. As its instrument of destruction, the bulldozer of its social engineering, the Court invents a boundless, and boundlessly manipulable, test of psychological coercion. Today's opinion shows more forcefully than volumes of argumentation why our nation's protection, that fortress which is our Constitution, cannot possibly rest upon the change-able philosophical predilections of the justices of this Court, but must have deep foundations in the historic practices of our people.

I

Justice Holmes's aphorism that "a page of history is worth a volume of logic" applies with particular force to our Establishment Clause jurisprudence. As we have recognized, our interpretation of the Establish-ment Clause should "comport with what history re-veals was the contemporaneous understanding of its guarantees." "The line we must draw between the per-missible and the impermissible is one which accords with history and faithfully reflects the understanding of the Founding Fathers." "Historical evidence sheds light not only on what the draftsmen intended the Establishment Clause to mean, but also on how they thought that Clause applied" to contemporaneous practices. Thus, "the existence from the beginning of the Nation's life of a practice, while not conclusive of its constitutionality is a fact of considerable import in the interpretation" of the Establishment Clause.

The history and tradition of our nation are replete with public ceremonies featuring prayers of thanks-giving and petition. Illustrations of this point have been amply provided in our prior opinions, but since the Court is so oblivious to our history as to suggest that the Constitution restricts "preservation and transmission of religious beliefs to the private sphere," it appears necessary to provide another brief account.

From our nation's origin, prayer has been a prominent part of governmental ceremonies and proclamations. The Declaration of Independence, the document marking our birth as a separate people, "appeal[ed] to the Supreme Judge of the world for the rectitude of our intentions" and avowed "a firm reliance on the protection of divine Providence." In his first inaugural address, after swearing his oath of office on a Bible, George Washington deliberately made a prayer a part of his first official act as president:

> [I]t would be peculiarly improper to omit in this first official act my fervent supplications to that Almighty Being who rules over the universe, who presides in the councils of nations, and whose providential aids can supply every human defect, that His benediction may consecrate to the liberties and happiness of the people of the United States a Government instituted by themselves for these essential purposes.

Such supplications have been a characteristic feature of inaugural addresses ever since. Thomas Jefferson, for example, prayed in his first inaugural address: "May that Infinite Power which rules the destinies of the universe lead our councils to what is best, and give

them a favorable issue for your peace and prosperity."
In his second inaugural address, Jefferson acknowledged his need for divine guidance and invited his audience to join his prayer:

> I shall need, too, the favor of that Being in whose
> hands we are, who led our fathers, as Israel of
> old, from their native land and planted them in
> a country flowing with all the necessaries and
> comforts of life; who has covered our infancy
> with His providence and our riper years with
> His wisdom and power, and to whose goodness
> I ask you to join in supplications with me that
> He will so enlighten the minds of your servants,
> guide their councils, and prosper their measures
> that whatsoever they do shall result in your
> good, and shall secure to you the peace, friend-
> ship, and approbation of all nations.

Similarly, James Madison, in his first inaugural address, placed his confidence

> in the guardianship and guidance of that Al-
> mighty Being whose power regulates the des-
> tiny of nations, whose blessings have been so
> conspicuously dispensed to this rising Republic,
> and to whom we are bound to address our de-
> vout gratitude for the past, as well as our fervent
> supplications and best hopes for the future.

Most recently, President [George H. W.] Bush, continuing the tradition established by President Washington, asked those attending his inauguration to bow their heads, and made a prayer his first official act as president.

Our national celebration of Thanksgiving likewise dates back to President Washington. As we recounted:

> The day after the First Amendment was proposed, Congress urged President Washington to proclaim a day of public thanksgiving and prayer, to be observed by acknowledging with grateful hearts the many and signal favours of Almighty God. President Washington proclaimed November 26, 1789, a day of thanksgiving to offer our prayers and supplications to the Great Lord and Ruler of Nations, and beseech Him to pardon our national and other transgressions.

This tradition of Thanksgiving Proclamations— with their religious theme of prayerful gratitude to God—has been adhered to by almost every president.

The other two branches of the federal government also have a long-established practice of prayer at public events. Congressional sessions have opened with a chaplain's prayer ever since the First Congress. And this Court's own sessions have opened with the invocation "God save the United States and this Honorable Court" since the days of Chief Justice Marshall.

In addition to this general tradition of prayer at

public ceremonies, there exists a more specific tradition of invocations and benedictions at public school graduation exercises. By one account, the first public high school graduation ceremony took place in Connecticut in July 1868—the very month, as it happens, that the Fourteenth Amendment (the vehicle by which the Establishment Clause has been applied against the states) was ratified—when "15 seniors from the Norwich Free Academy marched in their best Sunday suits and dresses into a church hall and waited through majestic music and long prayers." As the Court obliquely acknowledges in describing the "customary features" of high school graduations, the invocation and benediction have long been recognized to be "as traditional as any other parts of the school graduation program and are widely established."

II

I find it a sufficient embarrassment that our Establishment Clause jurisprudence regarding holiday displays has come to "require scrutiny more commonly associated with interior decorators than with the judiciary." But interior decorating is a rock-hard science compared to psychology practiced by amateurs. A few citations of "research in psychology" that have no particular bearing upon the precise issue here cannot disguise the fact that the Court has gone beyond the realm where judges know what they are doing. The Court's argument that state officials have "coerced" students to take part in the invocation and benediction at graduation ceremonies is, not to put too fine a point on it, incoherent.

The Court's notion that a student who simply sits in "respectful silence" during the invocation and benediction (when all others are standing) has somehow joined—or would somehow be perceived as having joined—in the prayers is nothing short of ludicrous. We indeed live in a vulgar age. But surely "our social conventions" have not coarsened to the point that anyone who does not stand on his chair and shout obscenities can reasonably be deemed to have assented to everything said in his presence. Since the Court does not dispute that students exposed to prayer at graduation ceremonies retain (despite "subtle coercive pressures") the free will to sit, there is absolutely no basis for the Court's decision. It is fanciful enough to say that "a reasonable dissenter," standing head erect in a class of bowed heads, "could believe that the group exercise signified her own participation or approval of it." It is beyond the absurd to say that she could entertain such a belief while pointedly declining to rise.

But let us assume the very worst, that the non-participating graduate is "subtly coerced" . . . to stand! Even that half of the disjunctive does not remotely establish a "participation" (or an "appearance of participation") in a religious exercise. The Court acknowledges that, "in our culture, standing can signify adherence to a view or simple respect for the views of others." (Much more often the latter than the former, I think, except perhaps in the proverbial town meeting, where

one votes by standing.) But if it is a permissible infer-
ence that one who is standing is doing so simply out of
respect for the prayers of others that are in progress,
then how can it possibly be said that a "reasonable dissenter could believe that the group exercise signified
her own participation or approval"? Quite obviously, it
cannot. I may add, moreover, that maintaining respect
for the religious observances of others is a fundamental civic virtue that government (including the public
schools) can and should cultivate—so that, even if it
were the case that the displaying of such respect might
be mistaken for taking part in the prayer, I would deny
that the dissenter's interest in avoiding even the false
appearance of participation constitutionally trumps
the government's interest in fostering respect for religion generally.

III

The deeper flaw in the Court's opinion does not lie in
its wrong answer to the question whether there was
state-induced "peer-pressure" coercion; it lies, rather,
in the Court's making violation of the Establishment
Clause hinge on such a precious question. The coercion that was a hallmark of historical establishments
of religion was coercion of religious orthodoxy and of
financial support by force of law and threat of penalty.
Typically, attendance at the state church was required;
only clergy of the official church could lawfully perform sacraments; and dissenters, if tolerated, faced an

array of civil disabilities. Thus, for example, in the colony of Virginia, where the Church of England had been established, ministers were required by law to conform to the doctrine and rites of the Church of England; and all persons were required to attend church and observe the Sabbath, were tithed for the public support of Anglican ministers, and were taxed for the costs of building and repairing churches.

The Establishment Clause was adopted to prohibit such an establishment of religion at the federal level (and to protect state establishments of religion from federal interference). I will further acknowledge for the sake of argument that, as some scholars have argued, by 1790, the term "establishment" had acquired an additional meaning—"financial support of religion generally, by public taxation"—that reflected the development of "general or multiple" establishments, not limited to a single church. But that would still be an establishment coerced by force of law. And I will further concede that our constitutional tradition, from the Declaration of Independence and the first inaugural address of Washington, quoted earlier, down to the present day, has, with a few aberrations, ruled out of order government-sponsored endorsement of religion—even when no legal coercion is present, and indeed even when no ersatz, "peer-pressure" psycho-coercion is present—where the endorsement is sectarian, in the sense of specifying details upon which men and women who believe in a benevolent, omnipotent Creator and Ruler of the world are known to differ (for example, the divinity of Christ). But there is simply no support for the proposition that the officially sponsored non-denominational invocation and benediction read by Rabbi Gutterman—with no one legally coerced to recite them—violated the Constitution of the United States. To the contrary, they are so characteristically American they could have come from the pen of George Washington or Abraham Lincoln himself.

Thus, while I have no quarrel with the Court's general proposition that the Establishment Clause "guarantees that government may not coerce anyone to support or participate in religion or its exercise," I see no warrant for expanding the concept of coercion beyond acts backed by threat of penalty—a brand of coercion that, happily, is readily discernible to those of us who have made a career of reading the disciples of Blackstone, rather than of Freud. The Framers were indeed opposed to coercion of religious worship by the national government; but, as their own sponsorship of non-sectarian prayer in public events demonstrates, they understood that "speech is not coercive; the listener may do as he likes."

* * *

The reader has been told much in this case about the personal interest of Mr. Weisman and his daughter, and very little about the personal interests on the other side. They are not inconsequential. Church and state would not be such a difficult subject if religion were, as the Court apparently thinks it to be, some purely personal avocation that can be indulged entirely in secret, like pornography, in the privacy of one's room. For most believers, it is not that, and has never been. Religious men and women of almost all denominations have felt it necessary to acknowledge and beseech the blessing of God as a people, and not just as individuals, because they believe in the "protection of divine Providence," as the Declaration of Independence put it, not just for individuals but for societies; because they believe God to be, as Washington's first Thanksgiving Proclamation put it, the "Great Lord and Ruler of Nations." One can believe in the effectiveness of such public worship, or one can deprecate and deride it. But the longstanding American tradition of prayer at official ceremonies displays with unmistakable clarity that the Establishment Clause does not forbid the government to accommodate it.

The narrow context of the present case involves a community's celebration of one of the milestones in its young citizens' lives, and it is a bold step for this Court to seek to banish from that occasion, and from thousands of similar celebrations throughout this land, the expression of gratitude to God that a majority of the community wishes to make. The issue before us today is not the abstract philosophical question whether the alternative of frustrating this desire of a religious majority is to be preferred over the alternative of imposing "psychological coercion," or a feeling of exclusion, upon non-believers. Rather, the question is whether a mandatory choice in favor of the former has been imposed by the United States Constitution. As the age-old practices of our people show, the answer to that question is not at all in doubt.

I must add one final observation: the Founders of our Republic knew the fearsome potential of sectarian religious belief to generate civil dissension and civil strife. And they also knew that nothing, absolutely nothing, is so inclined to foster among religious believers of various faiths a toleration—no, an affection—for one another than voluntarily joining in prayer together, to the God whom they all worship and seek. Needless to say, no one should be compelled to do that, but it is a shame to deprive our public culture of the opportunity, and indeed the encouragement, for people to do it voluntarily. The Baptist or Catholic who heard and joined in the simple and inspiring prayers of Rabbi Gutterman on this official and patriotic occasion was inoculated from religious bigotry and prejudice in a manner that cannot be replicated. To deprive our society of that important unifying mechanism in order to spare the non-believer what seems to me the minimal inconvenience of standing, or even sitting in respectful non-participation, is as senseless in policy as it is unsupported in law.

Equal Treatment for Religious Citizens—from *Locke v. Davey*

———————

Under the State of Washington's Promise Scholarship Program, students who received scholarships for college expenses could use the scholarships for any course of study except the pursuit of a devotional theology degree. Joshua Davey sued when he learned that he could not use his Promise Scholarship for that purpose. By a vote of seven to two, the Supreme Court held in Locke v. Davey *(2004) that Washington's exclusion of the pursuit of a devotional theology degree from its otherwise inclusive scholarship program did not violate the Free Exercise Clause. In his dissent (joined by Justice Thomas), Justice Scalia argued that the Free Exercise Clause does not allow the government to single out religions for disfavored treatment.*

We articulated the principle that governs this case more than fifty years ago in *Everson v. Board of Education* (1947):

> New Jersey cannot hamper its citizens in the free exercise of their own religion. Consequently, it cannot exclude individual Catholics, Luther-

ans, Mohammedans, Baptists, Jews, Methodists, Non-believers, Presbyterians, or the members of any other faith, because of their faith, or lack of it, from receiving the benefits of public welfare legislation.

When the state makes a public benefit generally available, that benefit becomes part of the baseline against which burdens on religion are measured; and when the state withholds that benefit from some individuals solely on the basis of religion, it violates the Free Exercise Clause no less than if it had imposed a special tax.

That is precisely what the State of Washington has done here. It has created a generally available public benefit, whose receipt is conditioned only on academic performance, income, and attendance at an accredited school. It has then carved out a solitary course of study for exclusion: theology. No field of study but religion is singled out for disfavor in this fashion. Davey is not asking for a special benefit to which others are not entitled. He seeks only *equal* treatment—the right to direct his scholarship to his chosen course of study, a right every other Promise Scholar enjoys.

The Court's reference to historical "popular uprisings against procuring taxpayer funds to support church leaders" is therefore quite misplaced. That history involved not the inclusion of religious ministers in public benefits programs like the one at issue here, but laws that singled them out for financial aid. For example, the Virginia bill at which Madison's Remonstrance was directed provided: "For the support of Christian teachers [a] sum payable for tax on the property within this Commonwealth is hereby assessed." Laws supporting the clergy in other states operated in a similar fashion. One can concede the Framers' hostility to funding the clergy *specifically*, but that says nothing about whether the clergy had to be excluded from benefits the state made available to all. No one would seriously contend, for example, that the Framers would have barred ministers from using public roads on their way to church.

The Court makes no serious attempt to defend the program's neutrality, and instead identifies two features thought to render its discrimination less offensive. The first is the lightness of Davey's burden. The Court offers no authority for approving facial discrimination against religion simply because its material consequences are not severe. I might understand such a test if we were still in the business of reviewing facially neutral laws that merely happen to burden some individual's religious exercise, but we are not. See *Employment Division v. Smith* (1990). Discrimination *on the face of a statute* is something else. The indignity of being singled out for special burdens on the basis of one's religious calling is so profound that the concrete harm produced can never be dismissed as insubstantial. The Court has not required proof of "substantial" concrete harm with other forms of discrimination, and it should not do so here.

Even if there were some threshold quantum-of-harm requirement, surely Davey has satisfied it. The First Amendment, after all, guarantees *free* exercise of religion, and when the state exacts a financial penalty of almost $3,000 for religious exercise—whether by tax or by forfeiture of an otherwise available benefit— religious practice is anything *but* free.

The other reason the Court thinks this particular facial discrimination less offensive is that the scholarship program was not motivated by animus toward religion. The Court does not explain why the legislature's motive matters, and I fail to see why it should. If a state deprives a citizen of trial by jury or passes an *ex post facto* law, we do not pause to investigate whether it was actually trying to accomplish the evil the Constitution prohibits. It is sufficient that the citizen's rights have been infringed.

The Court has not approached other forms of discrimination this way. When we declared racial segregation unconstitutional, we did not ask whether the state had originally adopted the regime not out of "animus" against blacks, but because of a well-meaning but misguided belief that the races would be better off apart. It was sufficient to note the current effect of segregation on racial minorities. Similarly, the Court does not excuse statutes that facially discriminate against women just because they are the vestigial product of a well-intentioned view of women's appropriate social role.

There is no need to rely on analogies, however, because we have rejected the Court's methodology in this very context. In *McDaniel v. Paty* (1978), we considered a Tennessee statute that disqualified clergy from participation in the state constitutional convention. That statute, like the one here, was based upon a state constitutional provision—a clause in the 1796 Tennessee Constitution that disqualified clergy from sitting in the legislature. The state defended the statute as an attempt to be faithful to its constitutional separation of church and state, and we accepted that claimed benevolent purpose as bona fide. Nonetheless, because it did not justify facial discrimination against religion, we invalidated the restriction.

It may be that Washington's original purpose in excluding the clergy from public benefits was benign, and the same might be true of its purpose in maintaining the exclusion today. But those singled out for disfavor can be forgiven for suspecting more invidious forces at work. Let there be no doubt: this case is about discrimination against a religious minority. Most citizens of this country identify themselves as professing some religious belief, but the state's policy poses no obstacle to practitioners of only a tepid, civic version of faith. Those the statutory exclusion actually affects—those whose belief in their religion is so strong that they dedicate their study and their lives to its ministry—are a far narrower set. One need not delve too far into modern popular culture to perceive a trendy disdain for deep religious conviction. In an era when the Court is so quick to come to the aid of other disfavored groups, its indifference in this case, which involves a form of discrimination to which the Constitution actually speaks, is exceptional.

Today's holding is limited to training the clergy, but its logic is readily extendible, and there are plenty of directions to go. What next? Will we deny priests and nuns their prescription-drug benefits on the ground that taxpayers' freedom of conscience forbids medicating the clergy at public expense? This may seem fanciful, but recall that France has proposed banning religious attire from schools, invoking interests in secularism no less benign than those the Court embraces today. When the public's freedom of conscience is invoked to justify denial of equal treatment, benevolent motives shade into indifference and ultimately into repression. Having accepted the justification in this case, the Court is less well equipped to fend it off in the future. I respectfully dissent.

The Scalia Family

BY TAYLOR MEEHAN

When I reflect on Justice Scalia's faith, I re-live the justice's funeral Mass. Thousands silently gathered. Each moment was deliberate, measured, unhurried. There were the sounds of Gregorian chant, the smell of incense, a respectable amount of Latin, and no eulogy—precisely as the justice would have expected. And though there were two bishops and dozens more perfectly ordered priests in attendance, it was the justice's son who celebrated the Mass. During his homily, Father Scalia remarked that "every funeral reminds us of just how thin the veil is between this world and the next, between time and eternity, between the opportunity for conversion and the moment of judgment. So we cannot depart here unchanged."

The justice had passed away a week before. A bitter pill that no one had expected. I happened to be serving as one of his four law clerks at the time.

Months earlier, I also happened to meet the justice's son, Father Scalia, at the invitation of a dear friend. We began meeting regularly to talk about Catholicism and occasionally succumbed to a pastry or two at the Heidelberg Bakery. These meetings marked the final chapter in my repeatedly derailed journey to join the Catholic Church.

Justice Scalia never mentioned these meetings; likewise, I rarely talked about my day job with Father Scalia. That's not to say that the justice had no role in my becoming Catholic. The opposite—he was central to it.

He did not evangelize in chambers. Nor did he leave his Catholic faith for Sundays alone. There was the picture of St. Thomas More. Letters written and speeches given. Trips to Mass on holy days of obligation. And that uncompromising abidance by his oath, sworn before God, to faithfully and impartially discharge his duties and to protect the Constitution.

Of course, the most visible sign of the justice's faith was his marriage to Maureen and their nine children. And it was that most visible sign that turned me toward the Church (at long last). I am most grateful that one of those nine children grew up to be a priest with the patience and fortitude to lead me to the Church. And I am similarly grateful for the image of the justice's family at the funeral Mass. It is what I remember most about that day—the battalion of Scalias processing through the Basilica. Together, they were strong and resolute, each of them cared for by their mother, brothers, sisters, sons, daughters, aunts, uncles, nieces, and nephews. They embodied the Catholic Church's teaching on marriage and children—a teaching that had long been a sticking point in my conversion and one that, in that moment, I finally understood.

As Father Scalia said that day, "We cannot depart here unchanged." I did not. Four months later, I joined the Church in another Mass celebrated by the justice's son.

In both life and death, Justice Scalia taught me much about Catholic life—to be unwavering at times, to live honestly and humbly, and to "be home for dinner!" (a regular admonition of his). I never sensed that the justice perceived himself as anything but an imperfect Catholic. But he was devoted. And that is what made him admirable, commendable, and dearly missed.

Taylor Meehan clerked for Justice Scalia during the Court's October 2015 term. She practices law in Chicago.

My Godfather Nino

BY MARTIN L. C. FELDMAN

Nino and I were the closest of friends for nearly thirty-five years. His faith was inseparable from the man. And he expressed it in every way that he lived his life; thought his thoughts; smiled with the Creator. For Nino it was "the Holy Ghost," not "the Holy Spirit." He preferred the Traditional Latin Mass. He would refuse Communion if he hadn't been to Confession.

It was an honor to be his good friend. And I have no doubt that God put us together. For years, over whisky and cigars and old cowboy movies, we had animated conversations about life, society, law . . . and faith. Catholic faith.

Nino knew that from the time I was a youngster in high school, I had felt drawn to the Catholic faith. He introduced me to C. S. Lewis—he loved how Lewis translated his deep faith into lovable humor. Of course, lovable humor and resolute faith defined Nino. We'd spend long evenings together talking about Lewis, St. Thomas Aquinas, St. Thomas More. We spoke of faith, this world, the next. Our discussions were often long and animated and intense.

But he never sought to convert me.

And then, on May 6, 2009, after nearly two years of study with then-Archbishop Alfred Hughes of New Orleans, I was baptized into the Catholic faith. Nino was my godfather.

When I asked him if he would be, he laughed and said, "Marty, I have been working all my life to get to heaven, and you're going to slip in right ahead of me!" Once, on our way to Mass, he asked, "Are you really going to go through with this?" I got very angry because I thought he was questioning my faith. He smiled, shrugged, and said, "You're going to hate Confession."

Nino's faith was as constant as his judicial philosophy. One night in my home in New Orleans we were talking about the challenges in society today, and I asked him, "Nino, do you think if you get to heaven you'll know what's going on here on earth?" He smiled and said, "No Marty . . . it's heaven!"

I miss him. He knows it.

RIP, Nino.

Martin L. C. Feldman has been a federal district judge in Louisiana since 1983.

God's Mercy

BY MARY CLARE SCALIA MURRAY

For many of us who mourn Antonin Scalia, the only way to comprehend the loss is to place it in the framework of God's plan and God's mercy. It is clear that God granted Dad a merciful death, as unexpected and devastating as it was; what was not immediately clear to me was how his life and his passing have worked God's mercy in the world.

Dad allowed his faith to show as a part of his public persona. But when we say that his faith was important to him, I suspect most Americans understand that to mean: he was Catholic, he went to church.

What Dad's (and really Mom and Dad's) practice of faith meant for us growing up was that we never missed Sunday Mass unless we were sick (in which case we'd better plan on staying in bed for the whole day), and that as a family we drove however far was necessary to find what Dad considered an appropriate liturgy. During the four years we spent in Chicago, our Sundays were especially adventurous: rather than walking ten minutes to our neighborhood church, Dad drove us thirty minutes to a city church led by Italian priests with accents so thick that it was hard to tell whether they were speaking English or Latin, or maybe it was Italian after all.

As a family we laugh about our liturgy hunting as an example of our father's inconveniently high standards and our strict upbringing. But Dad's approach gave us a framework for faith: we learned obedience to the Church and an acceptance of the basic obligations we owe her. We also learned that though worship is a deeply personal experience, it is built on centuries of history and tradition rich with meaning.

Faith in our home was strengthened by the intellectual exercise of understanding the teachings of the Church through reason. There were frequent conversations about sermons, good and bad, and about why the Church teachings made sense for all of mankind, why we should understand them as Truth.

It was a strict upbringing and expectations were high. (Let me be honest here—Mom is no pushover either! I'm pretty sure we have her to thank for not being allowed to wear jeans until 1982.) And like most children, I struggled against what I perceived as a lack of mercy in how we were raised. Like so many, I confused mercy with lenience or laxity.

As an adult, the unconditional love I had from my father was clear; his amusement and forbearance with every attempt I made to prove him wrong in one way or another (I was not often successful but never gave up trying; his smirk as he turned aside each of my arguments is my favorite image of him), his support of and

pride in all his children, children-in-law, and grandchildren through all their successes and failures.

The events following Dad's death were physically
and emotionally exhausting, but also spiritually re-
newing. The procession of thousands of Americans
through the Supreme Court as he lay in repose brought
many of us great consolation. As for the funeral Mass,
we really did start with a plan for a small, private Latin
Mass. He loved the Latin Mass, but as a family we recognized that the final opportunity to pray for him as
a Church should be shared with the large number of
friends and faithful who relied on him. The joy and
peace from the funeral Mass were a gift to us and to
many, who continue to respond to it.

Many people have expressed to us that our griev-
ing must have been more difficult because it was public. That may be, though of course we wouldn't know
the difference. But there's another side to the attention elicited by his death: the incredible outpouring of
sympathy from around the country, even the world,
wonderful expressions of affection for our father, stories of his friendships, and most importantly prayers.
All of this has allowed us to continue to grow in our
understanding of our father and in his daily exercise
of God's love—which is what mercy is. His ability to
form deep, lifelong friendships with people of diverse
views; his generosity and humility in reaching out to
others, to strangers, to people from all walks of life.
These are the fruits of my father's faith and of God's
mercy through him.

Since his death I have learned so much about my father's faith and how he lived it. This is the great mercy we have been given through our loss: that our love for him and our understanding of his legacy to us continue to grow even in death; that we grow in a new understanding of God's love through the words and memories of others.

Some of my friends have expressed this so beautifully in the Jewish tradition: may his memory be a blessing. It is that, and also a source of grace, and an opportunity to grow in faith. That must be for us the greatest part of his legacy.

Mary Clare Scalia Murray, a daughter of Justice and Mrs. Scalia, is a high-school German teacher and the mother of seven children.

Homily at the Funeral Mass for Justice Scalia

BY REV. PAUL D. SCALIA

The funeral Mass for Justice Scalia was held on February 20, 2016, at the Basilica of the National Shrine of the Immaculate Conception in Washington, D.C. It was attended by thousands of the justice's friends and admirers, watched by many thousands more on television, and celebrated by his son, Reverend Paul D. Scalia. Father Scalia's homily honored his father by describing the significance of Justice Scalia's religious belief in his life and reminding congregants that they were there, "as he would want, to pray for God's inexplicable mercy to a sinner."

We are gathered here because of one man. A man known personally to many of us, known only by reputation to even more; a man loved by many, scorned by others; a man known for great controversy, and for great compassion. That man, of course, is Jesus of Nazareth.

It is He Whom we proclaim. Jesus Christ, Son of the Father, born of the Virgin Mary, crucified, buried, risen, seated at the right hand of the Father. It is because of Him, because of *His* life, death, and Resurrection, that we do not mourn as those who have no hope, but in confidence we commend Antonin Scalia to the mercy of God.

Scripture says, "Jesus Christ is the same yesterday, today and forever" [Heb 13:8]. And that sets a good course for our thoughts and our prayers here today. In effect, we look in three directions: to yesterday, in thanksgiving; to today, in petition; and into eternity, with hope.

We look to Jesus Christ yesterday—that is, to the past—in thanksgiving for the blessings God bestowed upon Dad. In the past week, many have recounted what Dad did for them, but here today, we recount what God did for Dad—how He blessed him. We give thanks, first of all, for the atoning death and life-giving Resurrection of Jesus Christ. Our Lord died and rose not only for all of us, but also for each of us. And at this time we look to that yesterday of His death and His Resurrection, and we give thanks that He died and rose for Dad. Further, we give thanks that Jesus brought him to new life in Baptism, nourished him with the Eucharist, and healed him in the confessional. We give thanks that Jesus bestowed upon him fifty-five years of marriage to the woman he loved—a woman who could match him at every step, and even hold him accountable.

God blessed Dad with a deep Catholic faith—the conviction that Christ's presence and power continue in the world today through His Body, the Church. He loved the clarity and coherence of the Church's teaching. He treasured the Church's ceremonies, especially the beauty of her ancient worship. He trusted the power of the sacraments as the means of salvation—as Christ working within him for his salvation.

Although, one Saturday evening he did scold me for having heard confessions that afternoon. And I hope that is some source of consolation (if there are any lawyers present) that the roman collar was not a shield against his criticism. The issue that evening was not that I'd been hearing confessions, but that he'd found himself in my confessional line. And he quickly departed it. As he put it later, "Like heck if I'm confessing to you!" The feeling was mutual.

God blessed Dad, as is well known, with a love for his country. He knew well what a close-run thing the founding of our nation was. And he saw in that founding, as did the founders themselves, a blessing. A blessing quickly lost when faith is banned from the public square, or when we refuse to bring it there. So he understood that there is no conflict between loving God and loving one's country, between one's faith and one's public service. Dad understood that the deeper he went in his Catholic faith, the better a citizen and public servant he became. God blessed him with a desire to be the country's good servant, *because* he was God's first.

We Scalias, however, give thanks for a particular blessing God bestowed. God blessed Dad with a love for his family. We have been thrilled to read and hear the many words of praise and admiration for him, his intellect, his writings, his speeches, his influence, and so on. But more important to us—and to him—is that he was Dad. He was the father that God gave us for the great adventure of family life. Sure, he forgot our names at times or mixed them up; but there *are* nine of us. He loved us, and sought to show that love, and sought to share the blessing of the faith he treasured. And he gave us one another, to have each other for support. That's the greatest wealth that parents can bestow, and right now we're particularly grateful for it.

So we look to the past, to Jesus Christ yesterday. We call to mind all of these blessings, and we give our Lord the honor and glory for them, for they are His work.

We look to Jesus today, in petition—to the present moment here and now, as we mourn the one we love and admire, the one whose absence pains us. Today we pray for him. We pray for the repose of his soul. We thank God for his goodness to Dad, as is right and just. But we also know that, although Dad believed, he did so imperfectly, like the rest of us. He tried to love God and neighbor but, like the rest of us, did so imperfectly. He was a practicing Catholic—practicing in the sense that he hadn't perfected it yet. Or, rather, that Christ was not yet perfected in him. And only those in whom Christ is brought to perfection can enter heaven. We are here then, to lend our prayers to that perfecting, to that final work of God's grace, in freeing Dad from every encumbrance of sin.

But don't take my word for it. Dad himself—not surprisingly—had something to say on the matter. Writing years ago to a Presbyterian minister whose funeral service he admired, he summarized quite nicely the pitfalls of funerals (and why he didn't like eulogies). He wrote, "even when the deceased was an admirable person—indeed, *especially* when the deceased was an admirable person—praise for his virtues can cause us to forget that we are praying for, and giving thanks for, God's inexplicable mercy to a sinner." Now, he would not have exempted himself from that. We are here, then, as he would want, to pray for God's inexplicable mercy to a sinner—to *this* sinner, Antonin Scalia. Let us not show him a false love and allow our admiration to deprive him of our prayers. We continue to show affection for him and do good for him by praying for him: that all stain of sin be washed away, that all wounds be healed, that he be purified of all that is not Christ. That he rest in peace.

Finally, we look to Jesus, forever, into eternity. Or, better, we consider our own place in eternity, and whether it will be with the Lord. Even as we pray for Dad to enter swiftly into eternal glory, we should be mindful of ourselves. Every funeral reminds us of just how thin the veil is, between this world and the next, between time and eternity, between the opportunity for conversion and the moment of judgment. So we cannot depart here unchanged. It makes no sense to celebrate God's goodness and mercy to Dad if we are not attentive and responsive to those realities in our own lives. We must allow this encounter with eternity to change us, to turn us from sin and toward the Lord. The English Dominican Father Bede Jarrett put it beautifully when he prayed, "O strong Son of God . . .

while You prepare a place for us, prepare us also for that happy place, that we may be with You and with those we love for all eternity."

"Jesus Christ is the same, yesterday, today and forever." My dear friends, this is also the structure of the Mass—the greatest prayer we can offer for Dad, because it's not our prayer but the Lord's. The Mass looks to Jesus yesterday. It reaches into the past—to the Last Supper, to the Crucifixion, to the Resurrection— and it makes those mysteries and their power present here, on this altar. Jesus himself becomes present here today, under the form of bread and wine, so that we can unite all of our prayers of thanksgiving, sorrow, and petition with Christ Himself, as an offering to the Father. And all of this, with a view to eternity— stretching toward heaven—where we hope to enjoy that perfect union with God himself and to see Dad again, and with him to rejoice in the communion of saints.

Letter to Dr. James C. Goodloe IV

In his funeral homily, Rev. Paul D. Scalia quotes from his father's September 1, 1998, letter to Dr. James C. Goodloe IV, the minister who conducted the funeral service for Justice Lewis F. Powell Jr. at Grace Covenant Presbyterian Church in Richmond. Here is the full letter:

Dear Dr. Goodloe:

I looked for you unsuccessfully at the luncheon following the funeral yesterday. I wanted to tell you how reverent and inspiring I found the service that you conducted.

In my aging years, I have attended so many funerals of prominent people that I consider myself a connoisseur of the genre. When the deceased and his family are nonbelievers, of course, there is not much to be said except praise for the departed who is no more. But even in Christian services conducted for deceased Christians, I am surprised at how often eulogy is the centerpiece of the service, rather than (as it was in your church) the Resurrection of Christ, and the eternal life which follows from that. I am told that, in Roman Catholic canon law, encomiums at funeral Masses are not permitted—though if that is the rule, I have never seen it observed except in the breach. I have always thought there is much to be said for such a prohibition, not only because it spares from embarrassment or dissembling those of us about whom little good can truthfully be said, but also because, even when the deceased was an admirable person—indeed, *especially* when the deceased was an admirable person—praise for his virtues can cause us to forget that we are praying for, and giving thanks for, God's inexplicable mercy to a sinner. (My goodness, that seems more like a Presbyterian thought than a Catholic one!)

Perhaps the clergymen who conduct relatively secular services are moved by a desire not to offend the nonbelievers in attendance—whose numbers tend to increase in proportion to the prominence of the deceased. What a great mistake. Weddings and funerals (but especially funerals) are the principal occasions left in modern America when you can preach the Good News not just to the faithful, but to those who have never really heard it.

Many thanks, Dr. Goodloe, for a service that did honor to Lewis and homage to God. It was a privilege to sit with your congregation. Best regards.

Sincerely,
Antonin Scalia

ACKNOWLEDGMENTS

As with *Scalia Speaks*, this volume reflects the contributions of countless individuals.

We are indebted to Maureen Scalia for inviting us to work on these volumes, and to Eugene Scalia for guiding this project to completion. We thank the Crown Forum team, led by Mary Reynics and Gary Jansen, for their editorial expertise, and Robert Barnett for masterminding the arrangement with Crown Forum.

We are grateful to A. J. Bellia, Father Connor, Judge Feldman, Greg Grimsal, Kristin Linsley, Taylor Meehan, Mary Clare Scalia Murray, Judge Schiltz, and Rabbi Soloveichik for sharing their moving recollections.

Ed's research assistant, Yale law student Rishabh Bhandari, meticulously read through the entire transcript, and Mark Shanoudy of the Ethics and Public Policy Center provided valuable logistical support.

We thank Father Paul Scalia for his introduction (which Chris thinks is nearly as good as the introduction to *Scalia Speaks*), as well as for permitting us to reprint his extraordinary homily for Justice Scalia's funeral Mass.

We are especially grateful to Justice Clarence Thomas for his beautiful foreword.

Finally, we again thank our wives, Adele Scalia and Deborah Whelan, for their patience and support on this project and for the faith they share with us.

INDEX

ABOUT THE AUTHORS

ANTONIN GREGORY SCALIA was born on March 11, 1936, in Trenton, New Jersey, the only child of Eugene and Catherine Scalia. His father, who had emigrated from Sicily as a young man, was a professor of Romance languages at Brooklyn College. His mother, a schoolteacher, was one of seven children of Italian immigrants. He grew up in Queens, where he played stickball, rooted for the Yankees, and joined the Boy Scouts. He was valedictorian of the Xavier High Class of 1953 and valedictorian of the Georgetown University class of 1957. He attended Harvard Law School, where he earned high honors and was a Notes Editor for the law review.

While at Harvard, Scalia went on a blind date with a Radcliffe student named Maureen McCarthy. They wed in 1960. Scalia then studied in Europe for a year as Sheldon Fellow of Harvard University before working at the law firm of Jones Day in Cleveland from 1961 to 1967. He left private practice to become a professor of law at the University of Virginia from 1967 to 1971, and then served in a number of government positions: general counsel of the Office of Telecommunications Policy from 1971 to 1972, chairman of the Administrative Conference of the United States from 1972 to 1974, and assistant attorney general for the Office of Legal Counsel in the U.S. Department of Justice from 1974 to 1977.

He returned to academic life in 1977, joining the faculty at the University of Chicago. He was also visiting professor of law at both Georgetown and Stanford, and was chairman of the American Bar Association's Section of Administrative Law from 1981 to 1982 and its Conference of Section chairman from 1982 to 1983.

In 1982, President Reagan nominated Scalia to join the U.S. Court of Appeals for the District of Columbia Circuit. Four years later, Reagan nominated him to the Supreme Court of the United States, to which he was confirmed by the Senate, 98–0. Justice Scalia took his seat on the bench on September 26, 1986.

As a Supreme Court justice, Scalia articulated and exercised the interpretive methods of originalism and textualism. He established himself as a forceful presence on the bench, a vivid and compelling writer, and a gregarious public presence. One of the most significant justices in the history of the Court, he served for nearly thirty years before his death on February 13, 2016.

Antonin Scalia was married to Maureen for fifty-five years. Together they had nine children and dozens of grandchildren. He was a loving husband, a devoted father, a devout Catholic, and a proud American.

CHRISTOPHER J. SCALIA is the eighth of Justice Scalia's nine children. He holds a PhD in English literature from the University of Wisconsin–Madison and was a professor of English at the University of Virginia's College at Wise from 2007 to 2015. His political commentary and book reviews have appeared in the *Wall Street Journal*, the *Weekly Stan-*

dard, the *Washington Post*, the *Times Literary Supplement*, and elsewhere. He works at a public relations firm in Northern Virginia, where he lives with his wife and three children.

EDWARD WHELAN was a law clerk for Justice Scalia during the Supreme Court's October 1991 term. A graduate of Harvard College and Harvard Law School, he has also served as general counsel to the U.S. Senate Committee on the Judiciary and as principal deputy assistant attorney general in the Office of Legal Counsel at the U.S. Department of Justice. Since 2004, he has been president of the Ethics and Public Policy Center. A father of four, he lives with his family near Washington, D.C.